The Very Best Me

The Very

Published by

Tamar Books

Best Me

by
C. D. Urbach

FIRST EDITION
First Impression . . . November 1993

Distributed by
MESORAH PUBLICATIONS, Ltd.
4401 Second Avenue
Brooklyn, New York 11232
(718) 921-9000

Distributed in Israel by
MESORAH MAFITZIM / J. GROSSMAN
Rechov Harav Uziel 117
Jerusalem, Israel

Distributed in Australia & New Zealand by
GOLD'S BOOK & GIFT CO.
36 William Street
Balaclava 3183, Vic., Australia

Distributed in Europe by
J. LEHMANN HEBREW BOOKSELLERS
20 Cambridge Terrace
Gateshead, Tyne and Wear
England NE8 1RP

Distributed in South Africa by
KOLLEL BOOKSHOP
22 Muller Street
Yeoville 2198
Johannesburg, South Africa

THE VERY BEST ME
© *Copyright 1993, by* TAMAR BOOKS

ISBN:
0-89906-141-9 (hardcover)
0-89906-142-7 (paperback)

Printed in the United States of America by Noble Book Press Corp.
Bound by Sefercraft, Quality Bookbinders, Ltd. Brooklyn, N.Y.

This book is dedicated to

Bentzion,

a very special boy

who strives to be his very best

always,

and to

Elaine,

an outstanding woman

and a shining example

of what it means to be your very best,

no matter what.

Table of Contents

An introduction from the **start** of our stories!

Dear Readers,
The stories you'll be reading
Are different, as you will see
But as each unfolds,
The message is bold:
Who is the very best me?
None of us is the same
We have our own challenges, too
The lessons we're sharing
Are about caring
And doing the best **you** can do!

Sincerely,
Tali, Shira, Yehudis, Liba,
Ari, Dovy and Ahuva

The Very Best Me

Tali was going into fifth grade, and she could hardly wait. Summer vacation had been fun, of course, but the busy preparations before the first day of school always made going back seem so exciting! There were uniforms, books, briefcases, and all kinds of supplies to buy. Besides, shopping with Ima made Tali feel special and grown up.

This morning, Ima and Tali were shopping for shoes. Tali held on tightly to her mother's hand as they pressed through the crowds of people in the big shopping mall. There were so many bright and colorful displays everywhere! Soon they reached a large stand which read: **CHILDREN'S SHOES.** A kind saleswoman came over to measure Tali's foot.

"She'll need a size two," she told Mrs. Bloom. Then, turning to Tali, she asked, "What kind of shoes were you interested in?"

"Do you have black patent leather?"

"Of course. All the young girls have been asking for them this year." The saleswoman stood up and soon returned with pair of striking shiny black shoes.

"How pretty!" said Mrs. Bloom.

"I don't like them," Tali said promptly.

"Why not, dear?" asked the lady, puzzled.

"They're missing the gold buckle in the front. And it's supposed to say Little Princess on the buckle."

"We haven't got any of those left," explained the saleswoman.

"Well," said Tali, "*everyone* in school will be wearing Little Princess shoes. How can I wear *plain* patent shoes? All my friends will laugh at me."

"Tali," Mrs. Bloom said quietly, "Tami's your best friend, and she doesn't have them. And she certainly wouldn't laugh at you."

Tali pouted, her arms crossed. "I don't want these shoes. I can't go to school tomorrow without Little Princess shoes."

"Sorry to have troubled you," said Mrs. Bloom apologetically to the saleswoman. "Let's go then, Tali."

Mrs. Bloom sighed. Tali had such a cute, dimpled smile and endearing personality. Yet, she was always so worried about what others thought of her that she was seldom satisfied.

As they headed towards the escalator, Mrs. Bloom suggested, "How about a haircut at the beauty parlor on the first floor?"

She usually cut Tali's hair at home, but last June, Tali had complained that all her classmates thought that her haircut was unstylish. The truth was that no one had actually said anything about it, but since all of her friends had their hair done professionally, Tali was sure that they *must* have thought she looked awful.

"Okay," Tali agreed, somewhat more cheerfully.

Of course, she knew exactly what style she'd request. She flipped excitedly through the pages of a very large hairstyle book until she found the right one.

"This is it!" she said, tugging on her mother's sleeve. "This is what Mindy and Shira have. I lo-o-ove it!"

The hairdresser glanced at the photo and nodded. "Oh, that's a nice style," she said, "but your hair's very fine, and I'm not sure it's suited for this cut. You see . . ."

"It's what I want," interrupted Tali.

The hairdresser looked to Mrs. Bloom for approval. Tali's mother shrugged her shoulders with a tired smile.

"Well, then," said the hairdresser, "if you'd really like that, I suppose we can try."

Although the final results didn't much resemble that of

the woman in the photo, Tali was satisfied with her flattering new haircut.

A half hour later, they were walking back through the ground floor of the shopping mall. They passed the window of the shoe store, and Tali stopped for a moment. She gazed wistfully at the display, which had looked so promising before. Just then, the saleswoman who had waited on them came running to the doorway.

"I'm so glad you came back," she said. "I found our last pair of those shoes your daughter wanted. Here they are!"

Mrs. Bloom went inside and paid the woman, thanking her warmly for her thoughtfulness.

"Ooh, they're beautiful!" breathed Tali. She was so happy! With her hair trimmed neatly and her Little Princess shoes, she was all set for school. Or so she thought. It was not long before a tiny little voice in her head began to whisper again.

All the popular girls will be wearing Friendship bracelets, you know, and your pocket folders from last year are s-o-o-o dull. Mindy and Shira will probably have Lucky Duck pencils, too.

Tali and her mother spent the next two hours traipsing to nearly every store in the mall until Tali had gotten everything she *"needed."* It was dark outside by the time they drove home, and they were both exhausted.

The next morning Tali was so excited that she could barely eat breakfast. She looked perfect! She felt perfect! She had moussed and blow-dried her hair carefully. Her earrings were made of *real* gold. Her new white uniform blouse had an elegant blue trimming on the collar and sleeves. She was wearing her new Little Princess shoes and a Friendship bracelet on each wrist. She had two Lucky Duck pencils and a Lucky Duck sharpener. She was really ready!

She skipped gaily to school, wondering what her friends would think of the New Tali Bloom.

The first girl she noticed in the hallway was Shira. Shira looked wonderful. Her hair was done in the latest style, and she was wearing the same blouse as Tali, only with red trimming instead of blue. Her shoes had the Little Princess buckle. And she had four Friendship bracelets on her left wrist.

"Hi, Shira!" Tali called casually.

Shira spun around. She studied Tali carefully from head to toe. Then she made a face. "You're just a copycat," she declared. Mindy came up beside her, and the two of them linked arms and walked away together.

Tali thought that perhaps some of the other girls might notice her new look, but not one of them even glanced in her direction all morning. Later, as she sat forlornly at her desk during recess, a great big tear rolled down her cheek. Another one fell, and then she began to sob and sob and couldn't stop.

She felt a soft, warm touch on her shoulder and looked up. It was her close friend, Tami, who had overheard Shira's comment to her earlier. Tami didn't look a bit different than she always had. She hadn't even gotten new shoes or a haircut.

"I think you look terrific, Tali," she offered comfortingly.

"Oh, Tami," cried Tali. "I'm so embarrassed!"

"Don't be," said Tami. "A true friend likes you just the way you are. People aren't always kinder when you try to be someone else."

Tali wiped her eyes. "They'd like me if they'd only give me a chance! I *can* be just like them!"

Tami smiled. "You're wrong, Tali. They don't want that. Do you know what I overheard Shira saying to the other girls today? She said, 'What happened to Tali? She used to be the only one we could count on to be *herself*.' And Mindy said, 'Yeah, I liked the way Tali wasn't afraid to do and say what she felt was right!'"

"R-really?" asked Tali in disbelief.

Tami nodded.

"You mean they liked me better before? But — they always thought I didn't look nice. And they thought —"

"You're the one who decided that, Tali! You told this to yourself so often, you convinced yourself it was true!"

"They never really liked me," argued Tali.

"Well," said Tami, smiling, "I don't know if that's true. In fact, I heard a rumor that the choir heads are planning to ask you if you'll play piano for them this year."

"They are?" gasped Tali.

"Look, here's one of them on her way over here right now," Tami pointed out with a giggle.

"I'm lucky to have a friend like you," said Tali, squeezing Tami's hand affectionately.

"You have more friends than you realize," said Tami. "Because the best way to have friends is to *be yourself.*

People aren't just interested in your clothes or the *things* you have. They like your personality. They don't want you to copy them. They want the *real* you!"

"I'll try," promised Tali earnestly. "I'll be the very best me around!"

A Vase Named Shira

eople feel sorry for me. They shake their heads with pity and smile sadly whenever they see me. They tell my mother how smart and talented I was, how athletic and graceful I used to be.

Before.

Before the wheelchair, that is. Before those long months in the hospital.

Today I turned fourteen. I'm glad my birthday's in the summer, because I can have all the fun I want. No school work to spoil the day at all!

Anyway, last year on the first day of sleep-away camp, there was a big rainstorm. Our counselor had told us to stay inside the bunkhouse because the lightning was close by. We knew it was dangerous, but we'd been watching anxiously all afternoon and hadn't seen any lightning from our window.

After two and a half hours of just sitting on our beds and talking, we started to get restless. I thought it would be a good idea to borrow my older sister's tape recorder so we could all listen to some music. Aviva had even offered to teach us the latest wedding dance. So, since none of us had actually seen any lightning, we all felt it would be safe enough for me to make a quick run to the next bunkhouse.

No sooner had I left when a blinding zigzag of light crackled across the black sky. I saw it very clearly. I was near a tree, and I remembered hearing once that trees can get struck down by lightning. I dashed away from it and across the empty field as fast as my legs would carry me. As I neared my sister's bunkhouse, I heard a very loud clap of thunder. Another powerful torrent of rain poured down, and in my panic, I slipped on the muddy grass. The next thing I saw was the large tree right next to the bunkhouse, looming over me, heading downward.

Suddenly, the sky seemed all yellow, then black. Then, nothingness.

When I awoke several hours later, I was in a white hospital bed.

"Lightning struck the tree," the doctor explained to my parents. "Your daughter was hit hard, and she can't move the right side of her body now." He paused, and added, "She's lucky to be alive."

My mother was nodding sadly, I remember, as my father comforted us with quiet hopeful words. "*Baruch Hashem*, we still have our Shira," he said.

"It's like our beautiful, antique vase," he continued, turning to me. "It may have lost some of its fine painted finish when it fell, but it is still in one piece. It is no less valuable and precious in our eyes. Of course, had it shattered, we would no longer be able to use it. But hardly anyone notices the faded painting and to us, it is still as beautiful as it ever was."

Ima held back her tears as she said, "Yes, Abba is right. Do you understand what Abba said, Shira'leh?"

I smiled weakly.

I, Shira, was still a person, precious in the eyes of my parents.

The accident might have changed my outside, but my *neshamah* was still unharmed. My mind and heart were still fully ready to serve Hashem, just as before.

Of course, it wasn't always easy. Especially since I'd always loved dancing and sports. In the beginning, angry thoughts would fill my head. I'd think: Why me? Why did this have to happen to me? Why couldn't the doctors just invent some kind of medicine so I could dance again. Dance?! So I could walk and run.

Each time these angry thoughts took over, I'd feel more and more sorry for myself. Sometimes, I'd even speak angrily to the people around me. All my friends tried so hard to cheer me up, but I wouldn't let myself be cheered up. I'd say, "You don't understand. You don't know how it feels to be me right now!" And on really hard days, my patience would wear out completely, and I would exclaim, "Why don't you leave me alone?" Well, that's exactly what they did. They cared, of course, but they didn't know what to say to me anymore, so they just stopped coming to visit.

Over and over, I tried to remind myself of the beautiful vase my father had described that first day in the hospital. In my mind, I knew he was right. But I still felt as though I should never have been "dropped" in the first place!

One evening, as my mother was helping me into my pajamas, she said, "Did you know that Aviva has been phoning you every single day since you left the hospital?"

I nodded glumly.

"She's certainly a special friend," Ima went on. "Well, tomorrow you'll be able to speak to her yourself! Abba and I have decided that you deserve to have your own bedroom phone. This way, you can spend some of your time chatting, instead of — well, instead of sitting here and being lonely."

"Ima," I finally blurted out in a trembling voice, "I can't *do* anything anymore!" And suddenly, as if they'd been waiting for this very moment, the tears came. I buried my head in my mother's lap and sobbed and sobbed.

"Shira," Ima said, gently brushing a loose strand of hair away from my face, "you *can* do almost anything. Why, you can still read, play indoor games, write with your left hand, laugh, talk to people, sing —"

"No, no!" I interrupted. "It's not fair! I want to stand up and walk around on my own. I want to play basketball, to dance —"

"We can't change what was meant to be, can we?" Ima began.

"I was meant to be a dancer," I said bitterly. "I want to lead beautiful dance performances when I grow up, to raise money for *tzedakah*. That's a *mitzvah*, isn't it? That's what I always wanted to do. So why did this have to happen?"

Ima looked into my eyes, and was quiet for a moment.

"Life is full of surprises, I guess," she said finally. "Very often, we're so sure of our decisions and plans for our future that — well, we forget who the real Planner is. Being absolutely, positively sure about what we *think* is best for us doesn't necessarily mean we're right about what really *is* best for us."

"Well, there's nothing much else I can do for the world — in a wheelchair," I said sullenly.

"Shira," Ima said, "There are many things which you can do to help others. But right now the best thing you can do is to give us back our old Shira. Cheerful, smiling, 'look-at-the-bright-side' Shira. Remember *her*?"

"Hardly," I admitted. We both laughed softly.

"You know, it's interesting," Ima said. "You never hear anyone saying 'Why me? Why must *I* have such pretty eyes? Why must *I* be such a talented actress?' Or: 'It's not fair that *I* have such a great family!' When people think about their blessings, they realize how fortunate they are. No one complains when Hashem gives them an obvious blessing, because they *understand* that it's a good thing. The reason people complain about problems is because it is sometimes just too difficult to understand how their situation is for the best."

By now I was feeling much, much better. I admired Ima's special way of explaining things to me so that I really understood.

"But it always *is* for the best," Ima continued, "because Hashem doesn't ever make mistakes. So of course, if anything happens, it's meant to be. And Hashem wants you to be the best *you* can be — with the gifts you *have*."

"I'll try, Ima," I said, with all my heart.

"I know you will," said Ima hugging me tightly.

❦　❦　❦

Remember that I told you about people passing by, noticing me in my wheelchair, and feeling sorry for me? Well, when that happens, I think of two things. First I think about my wonderful family and friends whom I love so very much, and how lucky I am to have them.

Then I think about the Dial-A-Mitzvah project I started in my community. You see, people send me the names of lonely friends or relatives who can't leave their homes often. I have lists and lists of them. Every morning, I call as many of them as I can. We talk, laugh, share ideas and feelings with one another. I've learned so much from all my phone friends! And if someone sounds a little sad, I tell them about the beautiful vase — and about me. To be honest, there are times when I feel frustrated at my inability to do all the things I want to do. Still, when people look at me and shake their heads in pity, I say with a big smile, "But I'm happy!"

And the best part of all?

I really am!

"My Father Doesn't Live Here Anymore"

he telephone rang, and Pessy jumped. She fumbled for her watch on the dresser, and squinted in disbelief. Could it be? It was only 6:45 A.M.

"Hello?" She tried to sound alert.

"Hello. May I speak with Mr. Zyman, please?" The deep voice on the other end of the line was unfamiliar.

"Um, um . . . Mr. Zyman is not, um . . . available. Can I take a message?"

"No, no. I'd rather speak to him personally. When will your father be home from *shul*?"

"Um . . . my father doesn't live here anymore."

"Oh." The voice had a note of surprise. "I'm sorry. I — uh — "

"It's okay," Pessy interrupted, sensing his discomfort. "My mother will be up in a few minutes. Who is calling?"

"What? Oh, oh yes. This is Rabbi Press, your brother Ari's *rebbe*. I — I'll call back a little later. Thank you."

Well, she'd said it. It felt weird to say, "My father doesn't live here anymore." Maybe people would think her father wasn't living, *chas v'shalom*. Maybe they'd think he was in jail, or worse. Of course, he wasn't in jail, and her father was alive and well — in another city.

Pessy's parents had gotten divorced only four weeks ago, about the time she'd arrived home from camp. Pessy preferred not to think about it too much, but she was old enough to understand. Although it hurt sometimes, she knew it had to be this way, and that everything that happened was for the best. Ari, who was only eight and a half, didn't understand at all. He was in a turmoil and had been crying himself to sleep a lot lately. Sometimes, he would confide his feelings to Pessy. He was angry, hurt and confused, Pessy realized, but she didn't know how to help him. After all, she herself was only twelve years old.

But she knew why Rabbi Press was calling this morning. Last night Ari had confessed to her about the trouble he'd gotten into in class yesterday. It wasn't that he didn't like his *rebbe;* all the boys loved Rabbi Press. It wasn't boredom, either. Rabbi Press was a wonderful *rebbe,* whose lessons were always interesting. And Ari was a good boy, really.

So why was he such a troublemaker this year? Others may have wondered, but Pessy knew the continual mischief had a lot to do with Ari's mixed-up feelings. Most of all, Ari missed his father terribly. He couldn't concentrate well on his schoolwork anymore, and most of the time he didn't even feel like trying. He was angry about the divorce, although he wasn't quite sure exactly whom to be angry with. Getting in trouble seemed the best way to show everyone just how angry he was.

Just then, the tantalizing smell of fresh coffee reached her room. That meant Ima was up. Should she mention the phone call from Rabbi Press? She didn't want to ruin her mother's morning. Ima was always cheerful around her two children, and they had never heard her complain. Still, Pessy knew that Ima had a lot on her mind, especially now. School had begun only two weeks ago, and Ari was already being sent home with extra assignments for misbehavior in class. He'd even gotten a detention once for being disrespectful to his English teacher.

"Ima, did you see my *Chumash* sheet?" called Ari from his room down the hallway.

"No, Ari," came the reply from downstairs.

"I can't find it! Rebbe's gonna yell at me. I can't go to school without that sheet!"

"You're not staying home, Ari. Come downstairs and eat breakfast, so you don't miss the bus."

"My Father Doesn't Live Here Anymore" / 29

"But *yesterday* I lost my *Chumash* sheet, and Rebbe said that if it happens again —"

"Ari, you have exactly four minutes to eat. And I'd rather talk to you on the same *floor*. Hurry down, please."

Pessy reached the kitchen first. "Good morning, Ima," she said brightly.

Her mother smiled at her.

"Eeee-mah!"

"Downstairs, Ari," Ima repeated.

And then the phone rang. Pessy watched as Ima spoke into the receiver.

"Hello? . . . Oh, good morning, Rabbi Press . . . Ari — what? . . . Oh, I'm sorry . . . Yes, I understand . . . No, Ari didn't tell me . . . We'll pay whatever it costs . . . I'll try to review his *Chumash* sheets with him . . . uh, Ari's father doesn't live here anymore . . . No, we're fine." Ima was listening and nodding her head, the way you nod your head when you already know what the other person is telling you.

"Mr. Zyman lives in Montreal now. *Baruch Hashem,* we have everything we need. I'll try to help Ari get better organized . . . No, no, just your understanding, Rabbi Press. That's the greatest help of all . . . Yes, good-bye."

By now, Ari was standing in the doorway of the kitchen. "I'm in big trouble, right, Ima?"

Ima looked up. "Well, do you have about seventy dollars to spare?"

Ari looked so scared that Pessy felt sorry for him. "That — that's how much it costs for glasses?" he asked.

"For Yitzi's glasses, yes. Why did you break them, Ari?

It isn't like you to do things like that. You aren't obligated to pay for them, but I think it's the right thing to do."

"I — I didn't think they would break," said Ari.

"When you throw someone's glasses on the ground, there is a very good chance that they will break, Ari," replied Ima patiently. "You must have been very upset at Yitzi. Did he say or do something that upset you?"

"Yes," Ari said quietly. He flopped down on one of the kitchen chairs. He seemed relieved that Ima wasn't going to punish him.

Ima pulled a chair up to the kitchen table and sat down next to Ari. "So?" she prompted, sipping her coffee slowly.

"Yitzi's father told him about you and Abba. And Yitzi told the whole class. Everyone was bothering me about it, and asking me so many questions!"

Ima remained silent, waiting for him to continue.

"Then, Rebbe asked a *Chumash* question, and I didn't know the answer. It's not because I'm dumb; it's because I was drawing a picture, so I didn't hear the question. So Yitzi whispered to Moishy, 'He doesn't know 'cause he doesn't have a father to review with him anymore!' "

"I never liked Yitzi," mumbled Pessy, her mouth full of cornflakes.

"Let's not talk unnecessary *lashon hara* about any-one," interrupted Ima. "Now, Ari, finish your story quickly. The bus will soon be here."

"He wants to miss his bus," said Pessy.

"I don't know why, but I got so mad at Yitzi! I started hitting him before I even realized what I was doing — in front of the whole class, and in front of Rebbe! I guess I must have hit his face, because his glasses fell on the floor. I looked down, and the glasses were broken in a million pieces. The outside part was all bent. I — I didn't know what to do. Yitzi started crying, and Rebbe sent me out of the class."

Ari looked down at the floor, unsure whether or not to continue. "I guess Rebbe told you," he finished in a small voice.

"Yes, he told me," said Ima with a sigh. "Your busdriver is honking the horn, Ari. We'll talk more about it later."

"Do I *have* to go to school?"

"You certainly do," said Ima firmly, but not angrily.

"Bye, Ima," Ari mumbled reluctantly, sliding off the kitchen chair.

"Bye, sweetheart. Have a good day."

"Bye," called Pessy cheerily. She hoped Ari would have a good day, too.

"We're all getting used to this, huh?" Ima said, turning to Pessy. Pessy shrugged.

"I don't care what other people say about us," she said earnestly. "We love each other, and it's no one else's business what happens in our house. Right, Ima?"

"That's very true, Pessy," Ima said proudly. "I can see you're prepared to handle this well. I wonder how we can help Ari, though. Children can be so cruel to each other sometimes."

"A girl in *my* class actually asked me if our family goes to a psychiatrist now," said Pessy.

"Really?" said Ima, shaking her head. "I'm surprised. I had no idea what you children have been putting up with lately. So what did you say, Pessy?"

"Well, at first I felt like saying something *very* mean. Then I thought to myself: She probably doesn't realize that's a rude question to ask. So I decided to be very polite, and I said, 'No, we don't. But if we did, I don't think I'd want to tell you. That's a private kind of thing, and you could really embarrass someone by asking them about it.' "

Ima nodded approvingly.

"And you know what?" Pessy continued. "*She* was embarrassed. She even had tears in her eyes and told me she was very sorry."

"And you said — ?"

"I said it was okay, and that we were still friends."

"That was just the right thing to do," said Ima thoughtfully. "You gave your friend the benefit of the doubt, and you did not give in to anger — Oh! It's 8:45 already. My, how time flies when I'm enjoying a good talk with my only daughter!"

Pessy laughed. "Oh, Ima, you're my favorite mother!"

She slung her briefcase over her shoulder, zipped up her jacket, and left for school in good spirits.

❦ ❦ ❦

That night, Pessy and Ari sat in the living room, talking. Ima was at a wedding, and the house seemed empty and quiet. Pessy was curled up on the sofa, and Ari sat cross-legged on the floor beside her. Both were feeling very grownup, for it was already way past their bedtime.

"You really should pay for Yitzi's glasses," Pessy was saying. "After all, Ari, *you* broke them, not Ima. Seventy dollars is a lot of money, you know."

"But I'm only eight and a half," said Ari. He was trying to keep his tired eyes from closing. Staying up late was a rare privilege, and he was determined not to waste this opportunity!

"How am I gonna give Ima seventy dollars? I don't have any money — I'm only a kid!"

"I know that, Ari. But maybe we can think of a way you could earn the money."

"But it would take a very long time. Ima has to pay right away."

"So you'll surprise her and pay it all back to her. Can you imagine how proud Ima will be?" Pessy looked deep into her little brother's eyes.

Ari nodded, yawning sleepily. "Okay, but just one thing —"

"What?"

"Do you think — could we — well, no —"

"*What*, Ari?"

"Is it okay if we, well, if — I go to sleep now? My eyes are hurting."

"Of course, silly! Good night. We'll think of a good idea tomorrow. Okay?"

There was no answer. Ari was already fast asleep.

Early the next morning, there was a knock at the front door. Good-bye summer, thought Pessy drowsily. Sleeping-in days were over! She pulled back her curtains and looked out the window. Standing outside was Rabbi Press! She quickly put on her long robe and hurried downstairs to open the door.

"Good morning," Rabbi Press said. "Is Ari up yet?"

Oh, no, Pessy thought. Her mind was racing. What did he do *now*?

As though he had read her thoughts, Rabbi Press smiled and said, "I just came over to give him a ride to school this morning. I met your mother at the wedding last night, and if you two are anything like *my* kids, you probably stayed up until who-knows-when, right?"

Pessy nodded.

"It's hard to wake up early when you haven't had enough sleep. Why don't you tell Ari that I'm here, and I'll wait outside in my car. *Shacharis* starts in about ten minutes. Okay?"

Pessy nodded again. "Sure, I'll tell him right now," she said.

"Thank you, uh — what's your name?"

"Pessy."

Rabbi Press smiled. "Pessy, you have a *mitzvah*. Be well and have a nice day."

Ari was dressed and ready in less time than it had ever taken him. "Bye!" he called happily as he sped out the door.

At the breakfast table, Pessy told Ima about the unexpected visit.

"Ari's lucky to have a *rebbe* like Rabbi Press," remarked Ima. "Well, we've got to be on our way this morning. The box drinks are in the refrigerator — take one for lunch. Oh — I almost forgot. I have a meeting after work today, so I'll be home a little late, around six."

"Can Ari and I go out for pizza, then?"

"Pizza? What a nutritious supper! Well, all right, on one condition."

"No soda?"

"Right! At least a healthy drink, okay? Bye, Pes," she said, handing her a few dollars for the pizza.

Pessy heard the jingle of keys near the front door as her mother left for work. Ima had just begun teaching full time in a nearby high school. Now that Abba wasn't living at home anymore, she had to work to support the family. Pessy reminded herself of Ari's problem. How could he earn the money to pay for Yitzi's glasses? Maybe he could sell popcorn and lemonade in the park — but that wouldn't make much money. Even the toy sale they'd arranged in July had only brought in fifteen dollars, and in any case, there were no old toys and games left to sell.

She glanced at the clock; it was time to leave. Maybe her friend Malka would have a suggestion. Malka was always bubbling over with great ideas for everyone and everything.

It was Malka who greeted her first at her locker that morning. "Pessy! You're here! Listen, I have a great idea for our eighth-grade graduation trip. I thought of it when — "

Pessy burst out laughing. "Malka, you're too much. It's

only September! Isn't it a little early for graduation? Unless, of course, we need ten months to save up the money it will cost!"

"Oh, I have an idea for that too, don't worry. We can sell — "

Pessy put up both her hands in mock protest. "Help! Help! I'm drowning in your ideas, Malka. Seriously, I do need a good idea for something very important. You'll probably think of a solution in a second. Meet me here at recess?"

"Sure! I love a challenge," giggled Malka.

"Then you'll love the test you're about to take," said an older voice behind them. They spun around. It was Miss Lichten, their *Navi* teacher, on her way into class. They both grabbed their *siddurim* and followed her to their classroom.

The *Navi* test was indeed a challenge, and Pessy almost forgot about Ari altogether. She knew the answers, though, and felt confident as she placed her paper on the teacher's desk.

"Survived?" asked Miss Lichten, with a friendly wink.

"Yes," breathed Pessy, as if it had been a close call.

"Early recess, girls," announced Miss Lichten. "Take a deep breath and enjoy!"

Pessy rushed to her locker to meet Malka. "Malka, I have a problem and I need your help. My brother accidentally broke another boy's glasses. They cost — "

"Accidentally?" repeated Malka. "Are you sure — "

"Yes. Listen, they cost seventy dollars. I told him he should really pay for them, so — "

"Wait, he's a little kid, isn't he? Besides, I'm sure your mother will pay for them."

"Yes, and yes. But we want to figure out a way for him to pay my mother back."

"Oh, I see. Hmm . . . that *is* a tough one. Child labor is illegal, you know," Malka grinned.

Pessy sighed. "I know. That's why I need an idea. I can't think of anything."

"I have it! There's a really nice optician about four blocks from school. Everyone buys glasses from him. If Ari's friend's mother were to buy new glasses from there — that would be perfect!"

"Huh?"

"The owner's name is Mr. Spielman. Maybe Ari can help him out on Sundays, until he earns the money to pay for his friend's glasses. Well, is that great, or is that great?"

"Hmm," said Pessy, thoughtfully. "It's great! Thank you!"

"Oh, you're welcome. Anytime, Pessy!" chuckled Malka.

"I knew you'd help. My worries are over!"

"And so is recess," said a familiar voice. Once again, the two girls followed their teacher into class.

❁ ❁ ❁

Pessy and Ari were at Pizza Palace. The cashier was looking at them expectantly, "Two slices and what else?"

"I'll have a large Coke," said Ari.

"Uh-uh," Pessy interrupted. "We'll have two milks, sir. Please."

Ari looked at her in disbelief. "*Milk?*"

"I promised Ima," she answered firmly. "Now, down to business."

Ari groaned. "*Milk,* and now *business*? You're no fun!" he complained.

"Listen, this is important," Pessy continued quickly. "Here's how you can earn the money to pay for Yitzi's glasses. Mr. Spielman's Optical Center is right across the street. We'll ask him how you can help out around the store. I'm sure it won't be long before you have enough money to pay Ima back for the glasses."

"Two slices, two milks!" shouted a voice.

"Right here," said Ari. Pessy paid, and together they chose a table. They ate hurriedly and as soon as they were finished, they rushed across the street.

Luckily, the store was empty now. Mr. Spielman had just finished with a customer, and he looked up as they came in.

"Hello, kids! You look like Zymans. Am I right?"

Pessy nodded and walked over to the counter. "Mr. Spielman, we need your help."

"Anything for a Zyman," he said cheerfully. "What can I do for you?"

Pessy briefly explained what had happened to Ari in school.

"Oh, yes, Mrs. Weiss called me this morning about Yitzi's glasses. She wants to replace them with similar ones. Hmm . . . Those glasses will cost her seventy dollars — did you know that?"

"Yes," said Ari. "But maybe I could help you out in the store and earn the money. I want to pay for the glasses myself."

Mr. Spielman smiled kindly. "How old are you, Ari?"

"I'm eight and a half. Eight and three-quarters, almost."

"And three-quarters, eh?" Mr. Spielman's warm eyes twinkled. "That's a good thing. I have just the job for a boy who's eight and three-quarters."

"You do?"

"Why, of course. Can you count to a hundred, Ari?"

"Perfectly," said Ari.

Mr. Spielman turned to Pessy for confirmation.

"Yes, he can. I taught him last year, and he doesn't get mixed up."

"Good. You see these trays over here? I'll need them put in order once a week. Customers are always in and out, and I don't have time to put the trays in numerical order. I'd be able to serve my customers better if I could find their tray numbers quickly. Do you understand?"

"Yes," said Ari.

"Now, there are two sets of trays. The red trays are for new glasses, and the blue ones are for repaired glasses. So you'll need to put both sets in order. That should take about an hour altogether, each week. Let's see, at five dollars a week . . . well, in fourteen weeks you'd have seventy dollars."

"Oh, thank you, Mr. Spielman," said Pessy. "We really appreciate it. Thanks so much!"

"As I said, anything for a Zyman. Your father's always been a good customer here. Maybe I'll call him up and tell him what wonderful children he — "

"*No*," said Ari.

"What?" Mr. Spielman looked confused.

Pessy smiled weakly. "Nothing. I mean — our father doesn't live at home anymore."

"Oh — oh, I see. Well, then, I guess I'll just have to write him a letter, huh, kids?" He looked up at the big clock behind him. "Closing time! I'll see you on Sunday, Ari. Nine o'clock sharp, okay?"

"I'll be here," Ari promised.

❦ ❦ ❦

Sunday mornings were working out wonderfully. Ima always relaxed upstairs for a while on her day off, and Ari would be back home by the time she was downstairs. The next few weeks passed uneventfully. Ari's behavior in class had improved greatly since the day Rabbi Press had given him a ride to school. They had talked things over, and Ari realized that his *rebbe* was willing to help him in every way; all he asked in return was that Ari try harder to do well in his studies. It was a fair deal, and Ari found himself caring more about his learning.

Still, one problem remained. Whenever anyone teased Ari about his father, he lost his temper. He was the only one in the class whose parents were divorced, and the boys often made him the target of their jokes. That made

Ari angry. They were very wrong to hurt his feelings, but when he used his hands to fight back, it always led to more trouble. Ima tried repeatedly to prepare him with appropriate responses, but it was to no avail. The comments made Ari's blood boil.

"Ari's mother takes him to *shul* on *Shabbos*!"

"Yeah, and I bet his sister makes *kiddush!*"

"I'm not allowed to play with Ari anymore."

"Me neither, not after he broke my glasses."

"Broken glasses, broken home!"

Ari would listen for as long as he could stand it. Then, he'd jump up and punch the boy standing closest to him, or the one who had made the cruelest remark. He often confessed these incidents to Pessy, but she was never sure when or how to tell their mother.

One afternoon, however, Ari burst into the house, sobbing uncontrollably. Ima got up and rushed to the door.

"What is it, Ari? What's the matter?"

He buried himself in her arms, unable to speak.

Ima did her best to soothe him. "Come, sit down and tell me what happened."

"I . . . can't . . . tell . . . you," sobbed Ari.

Ima turned to Pessy. "Do you have any idea what might have happened, Pessy?"

Pessy shook her head. Even she had never seen her brother so upset.

"Tell me," prodded Ima gently.

"But — it's about — the secret," Ari blurted, trying desperately to stop the tears that kept on coming.

"It's okay," Pessy reassured him. "Whatever it is, tell Ima."

"Yitzi's mother saw me there and — "

"Where?" asked Ima.

"Pessy, tell Ima about the store," begged Ari. His little shoulders were still shaking.

"Well," Pessy began. "Ari really wanted to pay back the money you had to give Mrs. Weiss for the glasses. So Mr. Spielman, the man in the optical store, agreed to let him help in the back of the store once a week."

"I put the trays in order," said Ari, calming down.

"He said he'd pay Ari five dollars a week, and in fourteen weeks he'd have enough money to pay you back."

Now Ima had tears in her eyes. "Really, Ari? And you kept it a secret all this time? I — I'm so *proud* of you!" She hugged him tightly.

But suddenly Ari was crying again. His story wasn't finished yet. "Yitzi's mother saw me in the back of the store yesterday. She was there to pick up Yitzi's new glasses because that order had come in a few weeks late. She looked at me in an angry kind of way before she left."

"Where was Mr. Spielman?" asked Pessy.

"He was in the basement, getting something. His other worker was helping Mrs. Weiss."

"Ari," said Ima. "You came home very — "

"I know," he continued, his voice breaking. "Because Yitzi came to school today and told everyone that I'm a thief. He said his mother saw me stealing from Mr.

"My Father Doesn't Live Here Anymore" / 43

Spielman's store and that he's never, ever gonna talk to me again."

Ima and Pessy waited patiently.

"And then — another boy said that his mother told him that boys without fathers are always wild, and that he should never invite me to their house. All the boys were so *mean* to me, Ima!"

Ima sighed heavily.

"Oh. Here. I have the money," he said, pulling out fourteen crumpled five-dollar bills from his pocket.

Ima kissed him. "Thank you, Ari. What you did was very, very special. And I'm going to speak to Rabbi Press about this problem right away."

Within half an hour, Ima had kept her word. By then, Pessy had succeeded in diverting Ari's attention and lightening his mood. They were playing an exciting game of Monopoly, and Ari was winning.

"Everything's going to be okay," Ima announced as she put down the receiver.

They looked up from the board expectantly, but Ima only shrugged and said, "That's all I'm saying about it. You'll find the rest out tomorrow."

The next morning, Ari made sure to be in school early. He didn't want to miss whatever "surprise" his mother had discussed with Rabbi Press! He didn't have to wait long. Immediately after *davening,* Rabbi Press addressed the class.

"Boys," he began in a solemn voice, "someone you know is in prison." He paused and looked slowly around the room. Every boy was listening, wide eyed. "This person is imprisoned right here in our city," he continued gravely, "and for a crime which he did not even commit. Imagine! An innocent Jew — locked in jail. This Jew has been labeled guilty without being given a chance to prove his innocence. Boys, is this the way the Torah teaches us to judge others?"

A resounding "NO!" was the response.

"You're right, boys. And that is why I have requested special permission for this Jew to have a fair trial. Would anyone like to watch this trial?"

Hands went up all over the room.

"Good. I have arranged for the trial to take place right here — in our classroom!" Several gasps of surprise were heard. "I now call upon Ari Zyman, the defendant, to stand up here at my desk."

Ari's face reddened as all eyes turned towards him. Hesitantly, he made his way to his teacher's desk. Rabbi Press nodded reassuringly. "Good. Now —" He opened the classroom door slightly and whispered a few words to someone standing in the hallway. A tall well-dressed woman entered the room.

"Mrs. Weiss, you were kind enough to give of your valuable time to come here this morning. Please tell the boys what you feel they should know about Ari Zyman."

"R-Rabbi Press," she faltered. "I — you — weren't we going to have a little meeting?"

"This is it," answered Rabbi Press, waving his hand towards the twenty-seven boys seated at their desks.

"Well!" said Mrs. Weiss in an annoyed tone.

"Please," urged Rabbi Press politely. "Speak to them."

Mrs. Weiss looked uncomfortable. "Well, I don't like to hurt anyone's feelings, but I do think Ari Zyman is a mischievous little boy. His family is different. He hasn't got anyone to teach him right from wrong. Already, he's stealing from —" She stopped mid-sentence, embarrassed. "Uh, I'm sorry. I guess I shouldn't say all this in public."

"We already know," piped up a boy in the back. "Yitzi told us everything."

Mrs. Weiss gulped. "Yitzi?"

"About Mr. Spielman's store," said another boy.

Rabbi Press raised his hand slightly. "Sh, boys. Now, I will call upon —" Again, he opened the door. In walked none other than Mr. Spielman!

Mr. Spielman looked rather surprised. Rabbi Press spoke as if nothing was unusual. "Please, Mr. Spielman. Come, stand here next to our defendant, Ari Zyman. He has been accused of stealing from your store. Tell the court here—" he gestured to the other boys in the room "—if Ari Zyman has ever stolen anything from you. Has anything at all been taken unlawfully from your store? And if so, do you have any reason to believe that Ari Zyman is the thief?"

Mr. Spielman shook his head back and forth, again and again.

"No, no! *Chas V'shalom!* Ari Zyman? This boy is a wonderful young man. In fact, Ari worked for me for fourteen weeks, fourteen Sundays, to earn enough money to pay his mother back for well, for s-something she'd b-bought him," he stammered.

"It's okay," said Rabbi Press, smiling. "You can tell the boys what the money was for. This information is very important for our case."

"Well then," said Mr. Spielman, relieved, "Ari knew that his mother had paid Mrs. Weiss the seventy dollars it cost to replace her son's broken glasses. He came to my store the next day and asked me what he could do to earn the money. He wanted to pay it all back to his mother." He paused to catch his breath. "I said, 'Sure, I have work for you at the back of the store.' Ari was a good, hard worker! I paid him each week, of course, according to the deal we made."

Rabbi Press turned to Mrs. Weiss. Mrs. Weiss stared at Ari in disbelief. "Do you mean that you were— *working* there?"

Ari nodded his head. He was beginning to feel very awkward, standing in front of the classroom.

There was a long silence.

Mrs. Weiss looked as if she wanted to be *anywhere* but in this classroom.

"So why are you always starting up with my Yitzi?" she finally blurted out.

"I'm not," replied Ari quietly. "The boys tease me a lot about my family. And Yitzi says the most hurtful things."

"It's true," called a boy in the middle row. "Ari doesn't like to fight. He just gets mad when the kids say mean things such as, for example, that they're not allowed to play with him anymore."

"Boys," said Rabbi Press, stepping to the center of the room again. "I said that there was a *Yid* in prison for a crime he did not commit. Not only was Ari Zyman accused of being a thief, which he is not — but he was also accused of being a bad boy in school. We all know that Ari is a fine boy. Right, Mr. Spielman?''

"Oh yes," said Mr. Spielman, nodding emphatically.

"Right, boys?" The boys nodded, too. "Then let this be a lesson for all of us," declared Rabbi Press. "Never judge another person negatively. Causing an innocent person to suffer is a terrible thing to do. Judging others without all the facts is wrong. We must never ever fall into that trap. We don't want to hurt others, or to hate them for no reason. That is not the right way for us to act.

"Thank you, Mrs. Weiss, for coming to this very important meeting. Thank you, Mr. Spielman, for joining us as well." Rabbi Press paused for a moment and smiled. "And I thank both of you for your excellent acting. I think that you dramatically brought home the desired point to our boys. He turned to the boys. "Boys, I think we've done it! We've freed a Jew from prison! Isn't that wonderful?''

Everybody cheered. Even Mrs. Weiss and Mr. Spielman clapped, as a blushing Ari hurried back to his seat. Rabbi Press was watching him and smiling. Ari smiled, too, gratefully welcoming this long-awaited chance for a fresh start.

A Funny Story

She could make you laugh until your stomach hurt. Most of us loved her. Counselors dreaded her, but she came back to camp each summer anyway. Of course, that had a lot to do with the fact that her father owned Camp Keff. *Keff* means fun in Hebrew, and Liba Lehman certainly added to our fun. She had a funny remark for every situation, and she never missed a beat. Her lines were so witty that she'd have people laughing even when the joke was on them! Liba had been a favorite with the campers since she was little, because she was so cute. She had gorgeous green eyes and silky black hair.

This summer, Liba was in my bunk. The rest of us were almost twelve, but Liba had just turned eleven. I got to know her pretty well because we shared the same bunk bed — that is, whenever she finally went to sleep. Curfew for our bunk was 10 p.m. Somehow, Liba was usually missing when Devorah, our counselor, came in to check on us.

One night, Liba told our entire bunk to go wherever they wished and that she would "take care of things." Only I stayed behind to keep her company.

"Hi!" said Devorah, walking in.

"Hello!" said Liba brightly.

"It's eleven-thirty," said Devorah, looking at her watch. "Where is everyone?"

"Well," explained Liba, "the girls were complaining that even though I'm always late for curfew, I never get into trouble. So I told them that they could go bunk-hopping tonight. I stayed here, so you wouldn't get worried about them."

Devorah just stared at her.

"Oh, and . . " Liba put her arm around me, "Dassy's here. The others will be fine. Don't worry. I say, let's all go to sleep and enjoy the peace and quiet!"

"Liba," Devorah's voice was stern, "you need to ask permission for these — these night activities! It's *my* responsibility to make sure that —"

"Should I go get everyone then?"

"No, no," Devorah said quickly. *"I'll* go. You two stay right here. Do you understand?"

I nodded. Liba cupped a hand around her ear.

"What?" she asked.

"I said, *stay right here —*"

"Oh, okay. Right here. Now I understand."

Devorah shook her head and muttered something to herself. She turned to me. "Dassy?"

"I'll do my best to keep her here," I said honestly. "But you know Liba."

Liba laughed. "Yes, we've met before, haven't we?"

As soon as Devorah left, Liba started giggling.

"Don't tell me you're leaving," I said.

"I won't." She paused. "But if my bed is empty tonight —"

"Very funny. Who are you visiting this time?"

"Sh! Someone might hear. And it's top secret."

"Even from me?"

"Well, no. I guess not."

"So?"

"They're breaking out Color War this week. I'm going to the Specialty Bunk to get details!"

"Wait a minute, Liba. I kept you company tonight. Can I come with you, too?"

"Okay, but hurry. Devorah will be back with the bunk before we know it. Let's go!"

I liked being friends with Liba. She was always doing something exciting, and if you weren't too goody-goody to go along with her ideas, you had fun too!

We took the darker, windier path, so that no one would see us. Quietly, we slipped through the back door of the Specialty Bunkhouse and hid near the cubbies. We could see and hear everything, without being noticed. It was great!

"I have a complaint," said Mimi. She was in charge of Canteen. "Someone is taking nosh without paying for it!"

"That's perfect!" shouted Reena. She was the head of Night Activity.

Everyone was quiet. I guess they all wanted to know what was so perfect about that.

"It's a perfect breakout," Reena explained happily. "Tomorrow we'll announce that there's been trouble in the Canteen. Everyone has to chip in five dollars to pay for the camp's loss."

"We're gonna lose our campers with that idea," someone said. It sounded like the art counselor.

"Of course we won't," said Reena, "because after lunch, we'll make another announcement stating that the real culprits felt guilty and decided to confess. We're consequently giving all the five- dollar bills *back*."

"I don't know, Reena," said Mimi doubtfully.

"Wait, I'm not done yet. Each five-dollar bill will say: **Color War Is Here!** We'll write these words on all the bills while the girls are eating lunch. How's that?"

There were claps of approval.

"Okay, but what about the real problem?" Mimi asked.

"Maybe the breakout idea will really work," said the art counselor. "Maybe the nosh-nappers will really feel bad, and turn themselves in."

"Well, they won't have much time," said Reena thoughtfully. "After all, hungry nosh-stealers probably wouldn't miss lunch!"

Suddenly, Devorah burst into the room. Her face was flushed, and she was out of breath. "Have you seen Liba Lehman?" she asked. "And Dassy Braun?"

"Anyone else?" joked Mimi.

"It's not funny," said Devorah angrily. "I finally got the rest of the bunk to sleep, and now I have to find those two. It's past midnight already!"

That was our cue. We sneaked out as carefully as we'd sneaked in. We raced back to our bunkhouse as fast as we could, and dived under our covers. By the time Devorah got back, we were fast asleep!

The next morning at breakfast, Reena and Mimi made their announcement. Everyone was surprised — except for us, of course. Questions of "who" and "why" flew from one girl to another.

"Girls," said Mimi in a serious voice, "we had hoped that the girls themselves would admit their mistake and pay for the things they took."

"Yes," continued Reena, "that would have been the right and proper thing to do. But in the meantime, Camp Keff has lost hundreds of dollars in merchandise because of these girls." She looked around the room. "Therefore, each counselor is being asked to collect five dollars from every camper in her bunk. That is the only way we can cover this great loss."

"That's not fair!" shouted one girl.

"I'll tell my parents!" yelled another.

The lunchroom was in an uproar. Suddenly, Liba jumped up. "I know who did it!" she declared, standing on her chair for all to see. People turned around to see who had spoken.

"Liba knows who did it!" repeated Judy loudly. The word spread quickly, and within minutes, the room was hushed. You could hear a pin drop.

Liba's eyes shone with excitement. "At the count of three, the fattest girl in each bunk should please come up to the head table."

Everyone gasped. I couldn't believe my ears!

"After all, anyone who's been stealing hundreds of dollars of food is probably *fat*, right?"

Nechama, the Head Counselor, took over. "Excuse me," she interrupted. Liba sat down, smiling. "We will now begin *bentching*," said Nechama.

After *bentching*, each bunk followed their counselors to the bunkhouses. We were all supposed to give in our five dollars right away.

"I bet it would have worked," Liba told me as we walked down the path. "Don't you think so, Dassy?"

"I don't know, but it was funny," I answered.

Just then there was a big commotion behind us. We spun around. There was Henny, the heaviest girl in our bunk, surrounded by girls. Her face was tear-streaked.

"I didn't do it!" she kept repeating. "I didn't do it! I didn't do it!"

"Well, you're the fattest girl in the whole camp!" said a tall girl beside her. "You haven't stopped eating since you got off the bus!"

Some of the girls giggled.

"Uh-oh, Liba. Look what you started," I whispered to her.

"I'll fix it," said Liba. "Henny didn't do it," she announced. "Okay? I *know* Henny didn't do it."

Henny looked hopeful as the girls listened to what Liba was saying.

"One person couldn't have eaten all that nosh. She probably sold it secretly to the campers after curfew."

"I still think Henny did it," said the tall girl. "She's always eating."

Henny's eyes filled with tears again.

"I would never steal," she insisted, her voice trembling.

"Here we are," called Devorah. "Get your money, girls!"

There was a lot of mumbling and grumbling as everyone headed to the Main Room for First Activity.

"Hey, where's Chanie?" someone shouted on the way there.

"She was trying to find her wallet when we left," said the tall girl.

"My wallet is so thin, I could hardly find it myself!" joked Judy.

"Oh, there she is!"

Chanie was running to catch up with us.

"Sorry, Devorah." She handed in her five- dollar bill.

"Looking for just the right one to give away?" That was Liba. "So many to choose from, it's hard to decide!"

"Yeah, maybe Chanie's been selling stuff," said Temimah, who was Henny's best friend. "Like from the Canteen!"

"Don't be ridiculous!" Chanie said hotly.

By then, we'd reached the Main Room. Nechama was on stage, blowing her whistle for quiet.

"Today's First Activity is . . ." I didn't hear what came next, because Liba was nudging me.

"Dassy!"

"What?" I whispered impatiently. I wanted to hear Nechama.

"Isn't it funny how everyone takes me so seriously? I just wanted people to believe the whole thing, so they'd have no idea it was Color War."

"Hilarious," I said. Actually I thought Liba had gone a little too far this time. Funny is funny, until it gets other people into trouble. Henny and Chanie were being accused for no reason. Maybe the same thing was going on in other bunks, too.

". . . a volunteer?"

Nechama was choosing one girl from each bunk. Several younger girls already stood on stage, waving to their friends in the audience. Liba and I raised our hands.

"Bunk Daled — Temimah Klein. Bunk Hey —"

"Oh well," shrugged Liba. "Next time!"

That was another thing I liked about Liba. She never seemed to let anything disappoint her. She was always in a good mood, smiling and joking around with everyone. She didn't get insulted easily, either. Mean words just slid right off her. Then, I realized that maybe that was why she didn't understand about hurt feelings. She was sure enough of herself to ignore any unkind remarks that were said to her. Most people feel hurt once in a while, or at least embarrassed. Not Liba Lehman! She wasn't afraid of campers, counselors — even of head counselors! I just couldn't help but admire her strong, lively nature. I was drawn to it like a magnet.

I turned my thoughts back to the girls on stage. They had all been handed cards with different instructions. Each volunteer was supposed to do what her card said, for as long as possible. The cards said silly things like SNEEZE, JOG, HOP, etc. The winner was the one who was still going after all the others had stopped. Either you felt foolish, tired, or you were just laughing too hard to continue. It was funny to watch, too! Liba, naturally, had a line for everyone on stage.

"Hey, Ruth! Keep spinning around. Maybe you'll remember where you lost my towel!"

"Atara, the stage! You finally got on stage!"

"*Oi, vey,* Temimah. Henny needs you! Come back. You're all she has!"

There was a lot of laughing. The volunteers were funny and so was Liba. She seemed to know everyone in camp! It didn't take long before there were only four girls left, then two girls, and then . . .

"The winner is Shevy Baum, from Bunk Yud-Aleph!" Shevy was our table's waitress.

"She gets the week off!" shouted Liba. "And we get a *good* waitress!"

"Yeah!" Everyone in our bunk hooted in agreement. Shevy blushed, and hurried off stage.

Nechama asked for a new group of volunteers. This time, not one girl in our bunk raised her hand.

"Bunk Daled?" Nechama looked surprised. "Where's your camp spirit? One girl . . ." But no one volunteered.

I don't know about the others, but I just didn't want Liba cracking a joke about me in front of the whole camp. We were good friends, so she knew more about me than anyone else. But where was Liba anyway? I glanced around the Main Room. She was up there, on the stage! Nechama was facing the camp audience, though, and didn't see her.

"Last chance, Bunk Daled! Nobody? Okay, Bunk Hey . . ."

Meanwhile, Liba was right behind Nechama, imitating her every move. Girls chuckled guiltily as Nechama chose the other volunteers, completely unaware of her "shadow." Once, she turned around unexpectedly, and Liba nearly fell off the stage trying to copy her. Nechama noticed her then, and handed her a card as if nothing had happened. We all watched as Liba read her card, rolling her eyes and groaning.

"Ready, set, GO!"

All the girls started at once. Liba's card must have said **laugh,** because that's exactly what she did for the next ten minutes straight, without a stop! Watching her laugh and laugh made us laugh harder. The Main Room was very noisy! Of course, she won the round.

Second Activity for our bunk was basketball. We had a great game, and worked up a nice appetite for lunch.

Color War broke out as planned, and the camp was divided into two teams right away.

"I can't believe we're on the same team!" Liba hugged me.

"I guess they don't know we're friends," I said, grinning.

Lunch was followed by Rest Time, as usual. Color War preparations were not to begin until Night Activity, which was always after supper.

"Shevy gave me a dirty plate today," complained Liba as we walked towards our bunkhouse.

"I guess she felt bad," I said matter-of-factly.

"Oh, Dassy! You know I was only joking. That's the way I am. I think of something funny and I say it. I don't mean to hurt anyone's feelings or anything."

What could I say? After all, I laughed at most of her jokes, along with everyone else. I knew it wasn't always right, but I didn't know how to explain it to her. Besides, I thought, maybe she really *couldn't* help it.

"Liba, can we detour for a minute?" I said suddenly.

"Sure, where do you want to go?"

"Well, I just saw a dark figure crawl into the Canteen! Quick, I want to see who it was! Remember, Mimi said —"

Liba didn't need any convincing. In fact, *she* practically dragged *me* there! We went around to the side of the locked booth, and peeked in through the window.

"Do you see what I see?" Liba whispered excitedly.

At first, I didn't. Just then, there was a quick flash of black, and a tiny squirrel hopped onto a tall pile of boxes.

It was nibbling furiously on a chocolate-covered Haddar wafer! We both watched, fascinated, as the squirrel finished the whole thing!

"Look! He's opening a bag of chips!" Liba cried, squeezing my hand tightly.

"Sh! If he hears us, he'll get scared."

"Well, of all the nerve," said Liba. "That squirrel's stealing food from *our* canteen, and *we* can't disturb him!"

"He's hungry. Ooh, look how cute. Liba, let's tell Mimi and Reena. They're really worried about the missing food. They —"

"They won't believe the thief is a squirrel," Liba giggled. "If that little squirrel would only know what a commotion his little appetite has caused around here!"

We left the squirrel and hurried to the Specialty bunkhouse to share our fantastic discovery. All the counselors got a real kick out of it. Reena promised to update the rest of the campers at suppertime.

On our way back to our bunkhouse, an idea suddenly struck me.

"You're like the squirrel, Liba!" I said, turning to her.

"And you're *nuts*!" laughed Liba. "What on earth are you talking about, Dassy?"

"The squirrel was eating because it was hungry. What does he know about Canteen and asking permission! Meanwhile, his little meals cost the camp a lot of money. But is it the squirrel's fault? No, he doesn't know any better."

"Dassy, Dassy. Calm down, relax. Did you think that it was *me* in there, nibbling away?"

I stopped walking. I guess I hadn't been explaining myself very clearly. I started over, slowly and carefully this time.

"Liba," I said, motioning her to sit down next to me on the grass, "you said that it's impossible for you not to say a joke when you think of it. Right?"

She nodded.

"Even though sometimes the joke could make a person feel bad?"

She nodded again.

"You can't help it. But in the meantime, someone is getting hurt, you see? Just like the squirrel. He's hungry, he finds food, he eats. But the camp is losing money!"

"I get it," Liba said quietly.

I picked up a fallen acorn and offered it to her. "Still friends?"

"Yes," said Liba. "I'm glad you told me."

"You mean it?"

"Of course. I'll really try to be more careful from now on. I think I owe a few apologies, too. And this acorn — let's give it to Mr. Squirrel so that he knows that there's healthy food around here, too!"

"Right!" I agreed happily. "He can still eat, and you can still be funny. Only without —"

"Starting a WAR!" exclaimed Liba.

We laughed until our stomachs hurt.

No More Joiners!

My name is Yehudis.

I don't know who you are, or when you will be reading this. Perhaps by then, I will be a mother, with children of my own. Maybe even a grandmother! That is, if I decide to show this to anyone at all. I'm not sure yet. But I'm writing this all down because it's a story with a happy ending. And I think it could help others just like me. Well, just like I *was!*

First, let me tell you a little bit about myself. I'm the youngest of five children. All of my older brothers and sisters were married by the time I was eight, so I've always felt like an only child. My parents still think of me as the "baby of the family," even though I just turned fourteen! *Baruch Hashem,* my father's furniture business is doing well, and we live comfortably. My mother doesn't have to work, so I get to spend lots of time with her. She's always been there for me when I needed to talk about anything. I take violin lessons every Sunday, and my parents and I go out to eat once a week at a nice restaurant. I just started high school this year, and I do well in most subjects. Sounds like I have everything a person could want? Well, I didn't always see it that way. As a matter of fact, until last year, I was as miserable as could be.

Why? If you're a careful reader, you might already have guessed the answer. I didn't mention anything about friends, did I? That's because for a long time, I didn't have any. Not a single friend I could honestly call my own. And I wasn't the type to pretend that I had a million friends if I didn't. Only how I wished it could be true!

Ever since first grade, I was the girl nobody wanted to play with. If another girl had to hold my hand in a circle game, she'd complain that my hands were "wet." If someone had to be my partner in a line-up, she'd say she wanted the partner she had yesterday instead.

In the second, third, and fourth grades, it was no better. Whenever I'd walk over to a group of girls playing during recess, they'd shout at once: "No more joiners!" Each time that happened, I'd walk away sadly, wondering why they didn't want me.

Our fifth grade English teacher gave us lots of projects. Projects usually meant groups, and for me, groups meant trouble. To be invited to join a group — that was out of the question. Nobody *ever* asked me to be in her group. So I'd have to gather all my courage, and go over to someone myself. Quietly, I'd ask, "Can I be in your group?" The answers weren't always the same, but they all meant the same thing: No. It was either, "We already have four people," or "We don't live near each other," or "Ask so-and-so, I don't care." So-and-so would usually make up some other excuse, and I'd be left alone, the only unchosen girl in the class. The teacher would end up deciding which group I should join. I'd have to work with girls who hadn't wanted me. It was humiliating, to say the least.

In the sixth grade, our Hebrew teacher taught us a lot about *middos*. She often spoke about treating people kindly, not embarrassing others, and things like that. Of course, after lessons like those, all the girls would be extra nice to me. Somehow, I never felt better about myself, even then. After all, I didn't want people to be kind to me just for the *mitzvah!* I wanted them to like *me* for who I was, because they *really* wanted to be friends. The special treatment never lasted, either. To them, I was still plain old Yehudis, whom nobody needed. Once, I thought of being absent for a long time so that they might miss me and wonder how I was doing. I tried it for a few days, but my mother could tell I was fine, and she made me go back to school. It probably wouldn't have worked, anyway.

Seventh grade was the worst. If I didn't speak to anyone, no one spoke to me. Even the teachers paid little attention to me that year. If I didn't raise my hand for a question or an answer, the teacher might not have known I was in class! Day after day, I'd imagine myself as the most popular girl in the class. I'd daydream about being invited to everyone's houses, and being smiled at by all the teachers. Sometimes I'd feel sad and lonely inside, and sometimes I'd just listen extra well in class, and push those thoughts aside. But always, I'd ask myself the same question. Why, why, why? What *was* it that made others not want to be my friend? Was it the way I looked? The way I dressed? Did I say or do the wrong things? The harder I tried to understand it all, the less I understood. I was sad, confused, and oh, so lonely!

In the eighth grade, my parents had a private phone line installed in my room. At first, I was so excited! I'd spend hours doing my homework or reading right near the telephone, so that I wouldn't miss a call. Not one person called! No one ever asked me for my phone number, because no one ever felt like talking to me. Besides, there was plenty of time to talk to me in school. Only good friends called each other at *home*.

One night, I overheard my parents talking in the living room. "It's so quiet around here sometimes," my mother was saying. "I wouldn't mind if Yehudis invited some girls over once in a while."

"She's not a *teenager*, like the older girls were,"

my father said. "Remember how we'd have to *beg* them for the telephone? They talked on that phone so much, you'd never guess they *saw* each other every day at school!"

My mother laughed, but only a little. "I don't understand it. She's always neat and clean, just like Shiffy and Suri were. She's an average student, and her teachers have never complained about her behavior or anything."

"It's true," my father agreed, "and it's not healthy for anyone to be alone all the time. But we've never mixed in with our children's social lives before, and we didn't with Yehudis, either. Maybe we should have. I don't know. Maybe we can't really help her with this."

I was upstairs on the top step, listening to every word. As distressing as the subject was, it still felt good to hear my parents discussing it. I'm lucky, I reminded myself. I have parents who love me and care about me. It wasn't their fault I didn't have friends. They gave me everything and were always there for me.

The voices were getting quieter, and I could no longer hear what they were saying. They must have realized that I might still be awake. I tiptoed back to my room, and closed the door. I climbed back into my bed and lay back comfortably on my pillow. I thought about my parents' conversation, and about myself. Thirteen years old, and the only teenager around without friends!

My years in elementary school had passed with a lot of loneliness, it was true. And I had gotten used to it, in a way. But my heart ached. I desperately wanted friends. I wished I knew how to change things so that people would want to be my friend. . .

Oh, my *Tehillim!* I'd almost forgotten. I only said one or two *kapitlach* each night, but it always made me feel better. The words just seemed to be talking to *me*, and I found comfort in the pages of my *Tehillim*. I switched on my lamp, and opened to where the soft red string lay holding my place. קי״ט! It was the longest *kapitel* — just when I really needed to pour my heart out to Hashem.

I read each word slowly, and with feeling. I didn't understand all of it. The parts I did understand, though, I tried to say with even more *kavanah*. It must have taken me close to an hour. Then, towards the end, I suddenly heard myself reading the very words I was feeling!

It was *pasuk* צָעִיר אָנֹכִי וְנִבְזֶה פִּקֻּדֶיךָ לֹא שָׁכָחְתִּי :קמ״א, *I am young and shamed [by people], [and still] your mitzvos I have not forgotten.*

That was the whole *pasuk*. I held one finger near those words, and finished the rest of the *kapitel* with excitement. I read and reread those six special words to myself, over and over again. Dovid *Hamelech* was also not honored by others (before he became king, of course). He suffered a lot of shame and embarrassment during those long years, running away from Shaul. He, too, cried tears of loneliness to Hashem.

Wow!

I knew there had to be a message for me in those words, but what was it?

Of course I kept Hashem's *mitzvos. Shabbos, kashrus*,

tznius . . . but did I really, really keep *all* the *mitzvos* I could be perfecting every day, like greeting others with a smile, being quick to help someone in need, etc.? Maybe not as well as I could.

I decided there and then that I was going to change that. From now on, I was going to polish those two *mitzvos* until they shone! I would try until I was so good at greeting people properly, that the smile would come all by itself — without planning . . . until I was so quick to help others that I wouldn't have time to *think* about what I could be doing instead.

I closed my precious *Tehillim* and kissed its leather cover with special feeling. I could hardly wait until the next morning!

The first few days were very, very hard. I was so used to my old ways that it wasn't easy to change.

The Old Yehudis had walked into school each morning with her head down, too shy and self-conscious to say hello to anyone. The Old Yehudis would head straight for her locker, get her books, and go directly to class. She'd slide sullenly into her seat, and do exactly as the teacher instructed, without even looking around. Yes, the Old Yehudis was tired of feeling unliked and unappreciated, so she kept to herself. After all, no one could reject you if you never said two words to them.

The New Yehudis was different!

It took my last ounce of courage, but I smiled to every single girl I passed in the hallway. I said good morning to the girls standing near my locker. At first, I got the same reaction from everyone. Their eyes would open wide in surprise. Then, they'd answer hello, but quickly turn away. Some people were so shocked, they couldn't say a word! All this made my "job" even harder of course, because I knew that they were all wondering what on earth had happened to me. But I was determined not to give up. Each morning I'd greet everyone with a smile, no matter what. I knew Hashem was helping me, because within one week, people were actually greeting me *first*!

I can't describe the happiness I felt walking into school one Friday, in the second month of my experiment. No sooner had I reached my locker, than I was surrounded by three or four girls. They had come over to talk to *me*, and I, Yehudis, was in the center.

"Hi!" said Devorah, smiling. She looked happy to see me.

"Do you want to be a *B'nos* leader?" asked Tzirel. "I think you'd like it, Yehudis." The sound of my name was like music to my ears!

I was about to answer, when the bell rang.

"Wait, Yehudis. Don't go," said Rivky, touching my arm. She paused. The other two seemed to understand and walked ahead of us. "I just wanted to say that — well, it's so nice to have a happy Yehudis around!"

"Th-thank you," I stammered. "I-I don't know what else to say."

"Don't say too much, or we'll be late for class!" said Rivky, her eyes twinkling. "Just keep it up. It's worthwhile, believe me. Don't let anything or anyone discourage you, okay?"

I nodded shyly. I was probably blushing too, but who cared? I was going to have friends!

The second *mitzvah* was easier. Now that I was talking more before class, girls started asking me questions about what we were studying. It seems I had the best notes on every subject, because I'd *always* listened in class. I was even being asked to lend my notes, once in a while, either to help someone study for a test or just catch up on what she'd missed. I did become a *B'nos* leader with Tzirel, and there were plenty of opportunities to help in *B'nos* meetings every *Shabbos*!

Still, there were days when my feelings were hurt, even as the New Yehudis. Once, before the Science Fair, I offered to help a girl carry her science project to the auditorium. I know *I* would have appreciated it if someone had helped me carry my display the day before. But she just looked at me and said, "No thanks!" with a tone of voice that almost made me cry. I guess she wasn't used to people asking to help her. But I knew it wasn't *me*. I'd done the right thing, I reminded myself. I said, "Okay, see you!" as cheerfully as I could and walked away.

Rivky had the locker right next to mine. Can you believe I never even knew who my neighbors were? I really owe her a lot for her encouragement while I was working on the New Yehudis. After all, I hadn't really done all that much to win her friendship in the past.

I guess she'd taken my shyness as disinterest until now, and was happy to see that I really *was* very interested in being her friend!

One afternoon, when school was over, a very outspoken girl passed by and noticed the two of us talking near our lockers.

"So, Yehudis," she said, snickering, "you've come out of your little SHELL! Mind if we call you TURTLE for short?" She laughed loudly, and patted me on the back with all her might.

It hurt and I swallowed hard. This was a test from Hashem, I felt, and I wanted to do the right thing. Getting angry certainly wasn't right! I thought quickly.

"Turtle?" I said, pretending to be serious. "How about Peanut — or Egg? Something kosher, at least!"

Everybody burst our laughing. The girl who'd spoken to me laughed, too.

"Hey, it's nice to meet you, TURTLE — I mean, Yehudis. Forgive me?" Another hard pat on the back.

I opened my mouth, but Rivky spoke first. "She *shouldn't*," she said, glaring, "but she will, because she's a good *friend*. Now, leave my *friend* alone, please."

"Well!" said the girl, noticeably surprised. "So the slow turtle has a quick lawyer!" With that, she walked away.

Well, I could go on and on, but I've already told you that the ending was going to be happy. That's why I decided to write about it, remember?

Tehillim works! Hashem answers our *tefillos*. He really does! And *mitzvos* are wonderful. They help us become better people, *and* better friends.

And a friend is worth a lot.

A Home Away From Home

t's best if you don't cry," said his father stiffly as they drove away from the house. "You're a big boy, now. Show that you're strong."

Asher tried hard to make the tears stop coming, but they came anyway. He didn't dare look up at his father; he knew his face was streaked with tears. His eyes felt puffy, too.

They rode in silence for a while. Suddenly, his father pulled over to the side of the road, and turned off the engine.

"Look, Asher," he said straightforwardly. "It's not easy for me, either. But sending Mommy to Europe for medical treatment is going to cost thousands of dollars. I'll need to work long hours to make all that money. I won't be home very much to look after you, so —"

"But Daddy, I'm a big boy. You even said I am. I can take care of myself when you're away."

Asher's father shook his head and smiled a little. "A nine-year-old boy can't do all the shopping and the laundry and the cooking, Asher. You know that."

Asher sat up straight. "Oh, but I can, Daddy. When Mommy was home in bed, I did a lot of that stuff. Mommy showed me how to make scrambled eggs and macaroni. I remember what to do. I can eat that every day; I don't mind."

Asher's father cleared his throat, and turned on the engine. He checked the rearview mirror, and edged carefully into the right lane.

"Try it, Asher. It's a very nice place. I'm sure you'll like the people there. There will be lots of kids your age, too, whose parents are away. And I promise that as soon as Mommy's well again, we'll bring you home. Okay?"

Okay?! Asher thought, miserably. What was okay about Mommy being ill, and so far away? And now, he was going to live in a Children's Home with people he'd never met before! Daddy had said the treatment could take up to a year, until Mommy would be strong enough to return to

America. He'd probably be homesick most of the time. No — it wasn't okay at all!

"Well, here's the building, Asher," his father said at last. "I'll bring in your things."

It was a large silent building which looked as if it had been built many years ago. The bricks were a dull grey, and Asher thought he'd even heard a child crying inside.

Didn't Daddy care? Asher wondered. He seemed so calm and unaffected as he greeted a middle-aged woman standing in the doorway. Asher watched the two grownups converse from his seat in the car. Just then, his father motioned him over. Reluctantly, Asher stepped out of the car and walked slowly towards the building's entrance.

His father placed a strong arm around his shoulders.

"This is my big boy," he said, not without pride.

"Your father is really going to miss you," said the woman kindly. "It seems that he'll be traveling back and forth to Europe a lot, but I'm sure he'll stop in to visit you whenever he's in town."

She glanced at Asher's father.

"Of course," his father agreed.

"You'll be happy here with us, Asher," she continued. "Your father has given us clear orders to take good care of you," she added, smiling.

There was a warm twinkle in her eyes as she spoke, and Asher felt a little better, somehow.

"So, Mr. Rubin. Anything else we should know?"

"Hmm..." his father said. "Oh, yes. Asher likes

A Home Away From Home / 75

scrambled eggs and macaroni, isn't that right?"

Asher shrugged half-heartedly.

"Oh, our cook will be relieved to hear that!" said the woman, laughing. "Come on in, Asher. I'll show you around. Would you like to join our little tour, Mr. Rubin?"

"It sounds nice," replied Mr. Rubin, "but my flight leaves in forty minutes, and there's a lot of traffic."

He gave Asher a quick hug, and began to leave. Suddenly, Asher burst into tears.

"I want to go with you, Daddy!" he sobbed. "Please, don't leave me here!"

Mr. Rubin bit his lip, struggling hard to control his own emotions. He tried to mask the sadness he himself was feeling, with a strength that was difficult to maintain.

"I-I'll call you, Asher. I love you. Thank you for everything, Mrs. Hellman. I'll be in touch. Goodbye."

"Please, Daddy! Let me come with you!" pleaded Asher desperately, clinging to his father's arm.

"I'll be back, Asher," said Mr. Rubin, gently pulling himself away.

He really *doesn't* care, thought Asher, feeling betrayed. He watched, sniffling, as his father walked back to their old blue car. Without looking up once, Mr. Rubin turned the key in the ignition, and disappeared down the road.

Mrs. Hellman was not unused to such scenes. Still, her heart went out to each and every child. Handing Asher a tissue, she said softly, "Your father really cares about you, Asher. He's trying to be strong. For you."

Asher shook his head.

For me?! he thought, confused. Then why didn't he let me stay with him? After all, it had been Daddy's decision to bring him to the Children's Home. Daddy had driven him here today. His father had patiently explained the reasons to him many times, but it all made very little sense to Asher. He felt alone, abandoned and unloved. His heart ached.

"Mrs. Hellman?"

Asher turned to see a young boy walking up to them.

"Yes, Ami. What is it?"

The boy looked at Asher curiously.

"Akiva put the duffel bag in the wrong room," he said. "There are no empty beds in our room. Which — "

"No, no," interrupted Mrs. Hellman. "The room number I gave him is correct, Ami. Tell Akiva to leave the bag in your room."

"But — "

"We'll speak later, Ami. In the meantime, why don't you show Asher where he'll be sleeping? The bed near the window will be his for now. Okay?"

Ami nodded. "Of course, Mrs. Hellman." He paused, looking Asher over very carefully. "Oh, wow! A new boy, finally! What's your name again?"

Politely extending his right hand in greeting, Asher answered, "Asher. Asher Rubin." His mother had always said it was important to be courteous to others, no matter how one was feeling inside.

"I-I guess you're Ami," he added shyly.

"Yeah."

"Well, go ahead, boys," urged Mrs. Hellman. "I'll come around soon to see how you're doing."

Asher followed as Ami led him proudly to the room they'd soon be sharing. They walked along a wide tiled corridor, lined with doors on either side. Most of them were closed. The setting reminded Asher of a hospital floor. He thought about his mother. He had visited her in the hospital during her last few weeks in America. She'd been too sick to remain at home any longer. He'd really missed her being at home. At least then he could spend more time with her and feel helpful around the house. At the hospital, it was different. The hospital was several miles from their home, and Asher's father was only able to bring him there once a week, on Sunday afternoons. His mother was extremely weak, and the nurses were always worried that she wasn't resting enough. They often tried to hurry his visits, but Asher knew that his mother enjoyed his company and politely reassured the nurses that his mother was okay and that she wasn't over-exerting herself. It was true, really. He'd do most of the talking, while his mother listened interestedly, smiling or laughing at just the right moments. Once in a while, she'd ask a few questions about his studies in school. She was proud of how well he was doing, and always told him so. But Asher had spent many long quiet hours at home, too. Sometimes, his father would come home from work early just to be with him, and that took away some of the loneliness he was feeling. Together, Asher realized now, they'd made the best of the situation.

"I guess you don't like it," said Ami apologetically, pointing to the simple narrow bed near the window.

Asher jumped, startled at the sound of Ami's voice. He had been so engrossed in thought that he'd completely forgotten where he was for a few moments.

"What? Oh no, of course I like it. It's fine. I mean, a bed is a bed," he stammered, embarrassed. How long had his mind been elsewhere?

"Okay," said Ami, sounding relieved. "It's just that you were standing there, kind of staring at the bed, with this sad look on your face. I — I thought you didn't like your new bed or something."

"Sorry," said Asher. He didn't quite know what else to say.

"Aww, it's okay," said Ami, dropping comfortably onto his own bed. "I'm ten and a half now, but my relatives brought me here when I was nine. On my ninth birthday, actually. I didn't want to come here, either, believe me." He crumpled up a piece of paper lying on his pillow. "A letter from — hey, why don't you sit down? The bed is safe, trust me!"

Asher lifted his duffel bag onto his bed and sat down next to it. Ami watched thoughtfully as Asher lay one arm across the zipper of his bag, as if to protect it.

"You can trust Akiva and me," he said. "We never ever touch each other's stuff without permission. But, wait a minute! You know, I thought Zohar was coming back."

"Zohar?"

"Yeah. You're sitting on his bed right now. He's from Israel and the place he was staying at closed down. They didn't have enough money to keep it going, so they had to transfer all the kids to other places.''

"So Zohar was sent all the way to America?'' asked Asher, puzzled. "Didn't that cost a lot of money, too?''

"Well, first he was transferred to another Children's Home in Israel. But while he was there, his sickness came back and the people in charge of that Home didn't feel they could take good care of him anymore. So they sent him here,'' concluded Ami.

The word sickness reminded Asher of his mother, and why he himself was here. Obviously, he wasn't the only one in this room who'd been through a hard time. "How long has Zohar been here?'' questioned Asher.

"Um. . . about a year.''

"A year?'' gasped Asher. "You mean kids really have to stay here that long?''

Ami nodded. "I've been here for a year and a half already. Some boys have been here since they were three or four years old.''

"Why did Zohar leave?''

"Well —'' Ami hesitated. "I don't want to scare you or anything —''

"No, please. Tell me,'' said Asher.

Just then, a familiar face appeared in the doorway.

"Hi, boys!'' It was Mrs. Hellman. "As soon as Akiva's back, I'll talk to the three of you together about Zohar. Meanwhile, Asher, please unpack your things. Ami will show you which drawers are yours. The closet space is shared, of course.''

"But Zohar's stuff is still here,'' began Ami. "I-I

mean, I'll move everything, Mrs. Hellman," he added quietly.

Mrs. Hellman nodded. "Yes, I've brought a box here for his belongings. Thank you, Ami. You'll like Ami," she said turning to Asher once more. "We all love him."

Ami blushed. Mrs. Hellman smiled, and closed the door softly behind her as she left. The boys worked quietly for a while, not saying a word.

Suddenly Ami blurted out, "He really isn't coming back."

"Were you good friends?" asked Asher.

Ami's eyes filled with tears. "*Very* good friends." He picked up a model airplane and showed it to Asher. "See this airplane?"

"It looks pretty neat," admitted Asher.

"It took Zohar hours and hours of careful hard work to put this thing together, and paint it."

"It's pretty good," repeated Asher. It really was, he thought, looking at it with admiration. Projects with lots of little pieces and parts confused him. He preferred simpler hobbies, like stamp collecting and trading cards.

"Especially for someone with epilepsy," said Ami.

"Epilepsy? What's that?"

"Zohar was born with it. People who have it are normal, completely normal, except that they get seizures. Their bodies suddenly go out of control and they can't stop shaking. It's as if their bones and muscles start moving without any warning. Some seizures are worse than others."

Asher put down the shirt he was folding and picked up the crumpled piece of paper Ami had left on the floor.

"Is this letter from Zohar?" he asked, opening the crumpled ball.

"Oh, that's an old letter. You can read it if you want to."

"Dear Ami," Asher read aloud. "I hope that you and Akiva are fine. The hospital staff is nice to me, *Baruch Hashem*. Today my doctor told me I'll be able to leave soon. Maybe another few days here and that's all. The Children's Home agreed to pay for a very expensive medicine which may stop the seizures. The doctors say I am very lucky, because some parents can't even afford to get this new medication for their own kids! There's lots more to it, but I'll be seeing you soon, so I'll tell you when I get back. Thanks for taking care of all my things while I'm away. I'm so happy that we're roommates! Regards to Akiva. Your friend, Zohar."

Asher folded the letter carefully, and placed it on the desk.

"Why did you crumple it, Ami?" he asked.

"Why not?" retorted Ami. The sudden sharp tone in his voice took Asher by surprise. "I don't save anything. Nothing. What for? I don't even have the pictures anymore. Or the—" He stopped short, realizing he'd said more than he'd planned to say.

"Pictures? Of whom?"

"Oh, I may as well tell you." He put down the airplane, cleared a space on Asher's cluttered bed, and sat down.

Ami took a deep breath.

"Remember I told you that I came here on my ninth birthday? Well, in our family, we celebrated every special event with my grandparents. My mother always said that grandchildren and grandparents have so much to give one another. So we got together a lot. Anyways—" He paused, and looked at Asher. "If you're bored, or you don't really want to hear all this, let me know. Maybe you have enough on your mind today."

"No, no," Asher assured him. "Go on. You can trust me, too. I never tell a secret."

"Oh, it's not much of a secret here. I made such a fuss when they brought me. Crying and kicking and screaming — I'll bet the whole place was talking about me."

"I guess I wasn't *that* bad," mused Asher, grinning.

"Well, the whole thing was just such a shock for me. My grandparents had planned a very special birthday party for me. I'd been looking forward to it for weeks! My father even took a day off from work, and my mother was dressed in her *Shabbos* clothes. For me! I-I felt so special."

Tears began trickling down Ami's cheeks, but he went on. "At last, we were on our way. The roads were clear and the sun was shining down on us. Inside our old, brown station wagon was a family, a very happy family, on the way to my birthday party!" The tears were flowing freely now. "It was a terrible accident. I miss my mother and father very much. All the time."

"I know," said Asher softly.

"But saving all the pictures and memories of them only made it harder for me. I used to look at the photos a lot and it always made me cry. Whenever I used my father's pen I'd be crying, too.''

"So you threw away everything?''

Ami nodded. "Mrs. Hellman didn't understand at first. She thought I was wrong to want to forget them so completely. But I didn't want to walk around crying all the time. I'll always remember my parents, in my heart and in my mind. I loved them. I *love* them.''

"I think I understand,'' said Asher.

Just then, Mrs. Hellman walked in with Akiva. "Shall we come back later?'' she asked, noticing Ami's tearstained face and Asher's serious gaze.

Ami shook his head. "I'm okay,'' he said, wiping his face with the back of his hand. "Just . . . remembering.''

Mrs. Hellman nodded knowingly, and cleared her throat. "Boys, Zohar had a very strong seizure at the hospital yesterday. Apparently, the new medicine hasn't had a chance to work yet. During the seizure, he hit his head very hard on the floor and. . .''

She looked around the room to see how the boys were handling the news so far. Ami and Akiva seemed anxious. Asher held his breath.

"Zohar was flown to another hospital which specializes in treating serious head injuries.''

"Can we visit him?'' asked all three boys at once.

"I'm afraid not,'' answered Mrs. Hellman. "Zohar's not ready for company just yet. But we can all *daven for* him to have a *refuah shleimah*. And hope for the best.''

The room was quiet.

"We always have to thank Hashem for what we have. Right, boys?"

"*Baruch Hashem,* we are healthy and well," said Ami meaningfully.

Asher's head was spinning. This morning, he had been feeling unhappy and sorry for himself. He missed his mother and father painfully, knowing he wouldn't be seeing either of them for a long time.

Then, he'd met Ami, who had even better reason to miss his parents. Still, he thanked Hashem for being healthy and well. Even Zohar had sounded happy in his letter. "I'm lucky," he'd written.

"I have so much," thought Asher. "I'm healthy, and I have both of my parents. With Hashem's help, Mommy will be better soon, and Daddy will visit as often as he can. Mrs. Hellman is kind and caring, and I have two wonderful roommates. Besides, I won't be here forever, even if it may seem like a long time. Mrs. Hellman is right. We should all thank Hashem for what we have. Thank you, Hashem, for this home away from home."

Dovy Writes

ometimes, I wish I was the president. Or the mayor, maybe. Perhaps even the editor of a very popular newspaper, which everybody reads.

How else can I transmit my message to millions of people all over the world? It's something I feel, deep inside my heart. I want to share it with everyone I see. But who will believe me? They'll say: First, you have to be an old man with white hair and lots of experience. Then we'll listen to you — maybe. You're just a young boy. What do you know about life? It would be disrespectful to argue, so I suppose I'd quietly walk away. Oh, but how I want to shout it from the mountaintops! How I wish the winds could carry my words over vast seas and glorious lands! I want to sing from my heart over a big microphone that's hooked up in every city, on every continent!

Hmm ... I guess I must have gotten carried away, because my older sister just asked me to please quiet down so she can study!

Well, I've just read over what I've written so far. I haven't been very clear, have I? I've forgotten to introduce myself properly, and I haven't even mentioned what it is I'd like to tell the world! Pardon me, dear reader, as I begin again on a more formal note.

My name is Dovy Reingold. I am twelve years old. Actually, I'm still eleven, but my birthday is tomorrow, so I already *feel* twelve. I have three older sisters and four younger brothers, which works out quite nicely; my sisters help my mother with almost everything! Abba makes sure we boys have certain jobs too, though. I guess it's not fair for the girls to do all of the work, and the boys to have *all* the fun!

I have reddish-blond hair and bluish-gray eyes. My sister Rochel (the one who asked me to be quiet before) calls my hair color auburn, which always makes me laugh. To me, it sounds like "Ow, burn!" and my hair isn't fire red, so why should my hair be called "Ow, burn"?

Baruch Hashem, we're one big, happy family. Sure, we fight once in a while. I think most brothers and sisters do.

It's a lot more pleasant for everyone (including us) when we don't, of course, but we're normal! Abba learns in Kollel full time, and is a real *talmid chacham*. Ima teaches in the mornings, and gives art classes at home twice a week. I don't know how she does it all, but she somehow manages to have time for each one of us. She always has a listening ear. Very often, she'll say, "If you don't mind following me around the house, I'd love to hear how your day went." (Or why we brought home a bad report card, or a bad pet — whatever!). Abba learns at home after supper, and the beautiful *nigunim* he sings when he's learning add so much warmth to the family atmosphere! When Abba's not home, we're all usually doing our homework, playing or cleaning up with a music tape on in the background. There's not much time to think about being crowded or not having roller skates when there's always something fun and exciting going on in your house! Whether it's a puppet show by Shaya and Sruli, or helping Chaim and Chanoch build a tree house, no one, but no one, is ever bored at our wonderful little house on Meadowbrook Road!

My sisters, Rochel, Henny and Gitty, share the pink room, and all of the boys share the blue room. Actually, the girls' room isn't really pink anymore, and our room doesn't look blue no matter how hard you imagine it, but that's because the paint's completely faded. I guess it's expensive to paint a whole house over, and Ima and Abba don't have money for extra things these days. *Baruch Hashem,* we always have decent clothing to wear (thanks to Gitty's sewing, Henny's sale-hunting and *my* hand-medowns), and delicious food to eat. Ima says Rochel is going to make a wonderful wife one day, because she's really a terrific cook.

Well, I'm back. You didn't know I was gone. What happened was that, as I was writing about Rochel's cooking, I smelled some yummy brownies baking, and ran downstairs to get some! Boy, were they good!

I just reread what I wrote, and I see that I still haven't told you what this is all about. My *rebbe* always tells me that it's important not to get distracted, to stick to one thing at a time, until you're finished; I have to work on that! Rabbi Shayne is right. Abba said I'm lucky to have had all the best *rebbeim* in the *yeshivah* so far. Come to think of it, Abba's said that to *all* of us *every* year, so sometimes we wonder!

Oi vey, there I go again! Maybe that's why real mayors and presidents hire *other* people to write their speeches for them. That way, no one in the audience has to get up and say, "Your Honor, what is your *point?*"

What I want to say is: Everyone, *please,* be happy with what you have! The more you look around to see what other people have, the more you think you have *less!* The more you look around to appreciate what you have, the more you know you *have!* The less you look at other people's things, the more you'll see of your things. And the more you appreciate what you have, the less you'll look around to see who has more! If you have less, be happy with less. If you're happy with less, Hashem will reward you with more!

That is my message — more or less.

When Nobody Understands

Part One

huva stared at her reflection in the big oval mirror above her dresser. Frowning, she combed all of her hair over to one side, fastened a pretty lavender bow to the ponytail, and studied herself.

No, that won't do.

With an exasperated sigh, she removed her gold earrings, and replaced them with simple silver studs. She checked the mirror again.

It's no use. It's hopeless.

Just then, Adina, her twin sister, entered the room.

"Hi, Ahuva!" she said casually. She noticed Ahuva's distraught face at once. "Ahuva? What's the matter? Why do you look so upset?"

"I'm upset because this problem has *no* solution!" replied Ahuva, still gazing sadly at the all-too-honest mirror before her.

"What problem?" asked Adina.

"Why, just *look* at me!" said Ahuva, not moving from the mirror.

"What's wrong?" repeated Adina, earnestly confused. "Is it the new jewelry Bubby bought us?"

"See!" Ahuva almost shouted. She turned around to face her sister. "Bought *us*. Us, us, us! Everything is always us!"

Adina opened her mouth to respond, then thought the better of it, and said nothing. She knew her twin well enough to understand when to just keep silent and listen. Eventually, the storm of emotion would blow over, and Ahuva would explain herself more calmly. Neither girl spoke for several moments.

"Don't you ever feel that way?" Ahuva finally asked.

"You mean that everyone always buys us identical presents?"

"Yeah. But it's not just presents. People are always treating us as if we're exactly the same person! They expect us to like exactly the same things and —"

"What was *that*?" interrupted Adina, startled by a loud, rumbling noise coming from outside.

"Oh, it's Abba's car pulling into the driveway. The muffler fell off this morning and the noise is awful. But Adina, listen, this thing is really getting to me lately."

"Okay, I can see that. But what has the mirror got to do with all this?"

Slowly Ahuva returned to her stance at the mirror. By now, Adina was standing beside her and they both glanced at their reflections. The twins looked almost identical. They both shared the finely formed features of their father and the delicate fair coloring of their mother. The two blonde-haired, blue-eyed and ivory-complexioned girls were the envy of many of their classmates. Not only were they pretty, but they had lots of friends. Even the teachers favored the twins, for they were as conscientious as they were charming.

"See how alike we look?" Ahuva complained. "It's no wonder people are always mixing us up. Even our relatives have trouble telling us apart. So, I was trying to . . . well . . ." She stopped, suddenly feeling foolish.

"Unidenticalize us?" offered Adina grinning. Ahuva nodded. Then she shook her head.

"Yes, I was," Ahuva admitted. "But it won't work."

"Wait a second," said Adina. "Isn't it important to be happy with what we have, Ahuva? I mean, we look okay, *Baruch Hashem*. Why would you want to change anything?"

"Oh, you don't understand," said Ahuva glumly. "And no one else does either."

"Tehillah always comes up with good solutions,"

remarked Adina thoughtfully. "Maybe she can help."

"Tehillah. One of *our* friends. See Adina? Do either of us have any friends with whom the other one isn't best friends, also?"

"Hmm. . . Not that I know of. You're right. But I don't mind. So, we like the same people. That's okay, isn't it?"

"No. I mean yes, of course it's okay. But sometimes it's just too much."

"Too much what?"

"Too much of one person. I mean being one person. Being *like* one person, rather." She paused. "I'm not being very clear, am I?"

"Not very clear, no. I'm not sure I understand you." Adina looked hesitant. "Do you wish we weren't twins?"

"Well, it *would* solve the problem," said Ahuva, somewhat wistfully. "If I wasn't a twin, I'd probably have my own room, my own dresser, my own clothes, *and* my own friends!"

Adina swallowed hard. What was there to say? If there were a few long moments of silence, Ahuva didn't realize it, for she was lost in thought.

"Well," said Adina abruptly, "I guess you don't need *me* here." Then, with all the casualness she could muster, she added, "I'm going over to Tehillah's house to play Pictionary with her, and Tzila and Raizel. See you."

The door closed softly behind her. Hearing the gentle click, Ahuva looked up. Adina was gone. When had she left? Oh, but why did it matter? She chided herself. Why did she and Adina have to be involved in the same activities all the time? Why did they always have to tell each other where they were going? From today onwards, she resolved firmly, Adina and I are no longer twins. I'll pretend we're regular sisters who are totally different from one another. Yes! The more she thought about it, the better it sounded. After all, she mused, what could be wrong with pretending?

There was a familiar knock-knock-knock at her door.

"Come in," she said absently.

It was her father. Mr. Wein opened the door without entering.

"Hi, Ahuva." He looked around. "Where's Adina?"

"Adina?" she shrugged. "I don't know. Maybe she went to the store."

"The store?" Mr. Wein raised one eyebrow. "Weren't you two invited to Tehillah's house for a gala Pictionary game with her two cousins from Belgium?"

So that's where Adina went. She nodded. "Adina said she was going there. Now I remember."

"And you?"

"I was — I wasn't in the mood."

"Well then," said Mr. Wein gesturing towards the hallway, "how about keeping me company for a little drive?"

"A drive? In that noisy car?"

Mr. Wein laughed. "We'll drive it to the mechanic. The drive back will be nice and quiet. How about it?"

"Okay!" She smoothed her skirt, and checked the mirror one last time.

"You changed your hairstyle," he commented.

"Uh huh."

"Any particular reason?"

Ahuvah smiled her usual, winning smile. "In the car. . ."

"You want to talk in the car?" clarified Mr. Wein. "Why not? Let's go."

He stepped back as Ahuva sprinted out the door and down the stairs ahead of him. It was no secret in the Wein household that Mr. Wein was immensely proud of his two daughters. In fact, he praised them so heartily that Mrs. Wein would frequently remind the girls that their beauty and talents were gifts from Hashem. It was very important, she stressed, never to allow praise and popularity to bring conceit. The Wein girls had both headed Dance together, and loved to sing. Thanks to Mrs. Wein, they were also dedicated Chesed Club Volunteers in their free time. They had even started a *Pirkei Avos Shabbos Shiur* in their own home. "Just to keep us on the right track," they had told their mother.

Mr. Wein was jolted out of his pleasant reverie by Ahuva's favorite ploy. She would often slip into the driver's seat, and honk the horn to the rhythm of the song "אֲחַכֶּה לּוֹ". Hurriedly, the awaited party would leave the house! He was downstairs in no time.

"I'm here," he said good-naturedly, turning the key in the ignition. "So. What's up?" He began driving at an exaggeratedly slow pace, so as not to upset the neighbors with the annoying noise of the muffler.

Ahuva unfastened the big lavender bow, ran her fingers through her fine blonde hair, and faced her father.

"Do I look like Adina?"

"Why yes, very much."

"I do? We don't look at all different?"

"Well, let me see." He glanced briefly in her direction. "Perhaps your eyes have a more lively exuberant shine. Adina's eyes are a deeper blue, more serene and peaceful. Both very pretty, of course."

"Anything else?" Ahuva asked hopefully.

Mr. Wein laughed. "If I don't keep my eyes on the road, we'll be going to the mechanic for a lot more than a new muffler, you know. What's on your mind?"

"I guess the eyes tell a lot about a person."

"How is that?"

"Well, Adina *is* more peaceful and serene than I am. She's a very content person. I'm more competitive."

"So?"

"And less content," she sighed.

Mr. Wein seemed surprised. "Really? I never noticed that. I've always been so impressed with my two shining, smiling daughters. Have I missed something along the way?"

"I don't know. I think it started when we both turned *bas mitzvah*."

"*Bas mitzvah*? That was almost three years ago. Have you really been miserable since then, Ahuva?"

"Well, not miserable exactly — "

Mr. Wein cleared his throat. "Can I call time-out? We're getting a lot of stares here. It's hard for me to concentrate. Let's get this noisy car to the garage first. Then I can give you the full attention you deserve."

"Okay, Dad."

One hour later, they were walking home from the repair shop. Apparently, the mechanic could not replace the muffler until the following morning. Mr. Wein had opted to leave the car there overnight; driving it in public had proven to be more embarrassing than he'd anticipated!

"Back to you, Ahuva."

She took a deep breath. "*Bas mitzvah* is the time when a Jewish girl becomes responsible for the *mitzvos* in the Torah. Right?"

"So far so good."

"She becomes a young woman in her own right, accountable for all of her deeds. It's a time when a girl resolves to really try and reach her full potential —"

"That's positive thinking, Ahuva. Hmm. . . I'll never forget the beautiful *melaveh malkah* Mom arranged for your *bas mitzvah*. We were so proud of you both!"

"Thanks, Dad, and this is going to sound terribly selfish and ungrateful, but do you know what? While Adina and I were sitting at the head of the table, wearing identical dresses, identical hairstyles and unwrapping all those identical presents, do you know what I was thinking?"

"Uh oh."

"I thought, I wish it could be just *me* celebrating my *bas mitzvah*, just me wearing my brand-new *Shabbos* dress, and — I'm ashamed of this Dad, but — just me getting all those lovely presents."

Mr. Wein let out a low whistle. "Well! You've taken me a little by surprise. Do you think your friends favored

Adina over you, perhaps?"

"Oh no, we've had the same friends for years. I'm sure they like us equally." She paused. "That's kind of the problem, though."

"My, oh my," said her father, shaking his head. "I've always felt that being twins was such a unique opportunity. After all, Mom's a twin, and you know how especially close she feels towards Aunt Sheila."

"But, Dad—"

"Listen, honey. You and Adina have a lot going for you, and—"

"And you just don't think it's right to complain."

"I guess not, no. I'm sorry, sweetheart."

Ahuva tried to hide her frustration, but it was difficult indeed.

"Well, we're home," said Mr. Wein resignedly. "And look who's — Adina! Hello, hello! Ahuva and I were just —"

"Just wondering how the game was going," interrupted Ahuva quickly. She didn't feel that she had the emotional strength to discuss the issue anymore.

Adina's face was flushed and rosy. "Oh, it was so much fun! We laughed so hard — Ahuva, you'd have *loved* it! I really wanted you to come, but you—"

"It's all right," said Ahuva, with a nonchalance she didn't feel.

"Tzila and Raizel *really* wanted to meet you," Adina went on cheerfully. "They said they'd heard so much about the Wein twins. They kept on asking me if we're really identical and—"

"Oh, I'm so *tired* of everyone's dumb questions!" blurted Ahuva.

Suddenly, she was sobbing. Mr. Wein and Adina watched, puzzled, as she tore away from them and ran into the house. There was sympathy in their eyes, but neither of them could find words to express the way they were feeling. Was it hurt, perhaps? Silently, Mr. Wein took Adina's hand, and together they went inside.

❧ ❧ ❧

Part Two

Did I cry myself to sleep? Ahuva wondered, blinking sleepily. That's funny; it's still dark outside. What time is it? Her alarm clock showed eight-thirty. Was it a dark morning, or was it evening? She sat up in bed, noticing the wrinkled clothes she was wearing. She vaguely remembered going downstairs several hours ago, and throwing herself on her bed, weeping loudly. There was a cold cup of tea and a few cookies on a plate near her bed. Mom must have brought that. She couldn't recall anyone coming in, though. "Boy, am I ever hungry," she thought now. "Hope there's still some supper left for me."

She got up slowly, still feeling a bit groggy from her nap, and washed *negel-vasser* in the adjoining washroom. Then, she walked over to the huge walk-in closet she and Adina shared. Since they both wore the same size and had similar tastes, they both had plenty of clothes. Mrs. Wein allowed a certain number of outfits to be purchased when necessary, and when combined, they each had a double wardrobe! Today, however, Ahuva pushed aside one outfit after another. Can't I wear something Adina hasn't worn? I'll ask Mom for the credit card. I need something new and different! In the meantime, she chose a flare denim skirt and yellow sweatshirt and scurried downstairs. She found only her mother in the kitchen, clearing the dishes from the table.

"Mom?"

Mrs. Wein looked up and smiled. "Well, good morning! Or should I say good evening?" She put the dishes in the sink and turned on the water. "Feeling any better?"

Ahuva nodded. "I guess."

"There's some spaghetti and meatballs left in that pot on the stove. Just warm it up, and have some salad with it. The salad's in the frig."

Ahuva didn't move. She seemed glued to her spot at the doorway of the kitchen.

"What's the matter, honey? Don't you like spaghetti and meatballs? I made it especially for you and Adina, since you two always ask me for it."

"No, thank you."

"Some salad, then? You must be hungry."

"What kind?"

"Why, vegetable salad, of course."

Ahuva shook her head. "No, thanks. I'll just make myself a tuna fish sandwich."

Mrs. Wein turned off the water and walked over to

the place where Ahuva was standing, as if in a trance. She felt her forehead with the back of her hand.

"You okay?" she asked, concerned.

"I'm fine. But Mom? Next time you go shopping, could you buy lots of tuna, please?"

Mrs. Wein looked into her daughter's eyes. She always claimed she could tell whether her children were sick or healthy by examining their eyes.

"Hmm. . . you seem okay. What? Sure I can buy tuna. I'll buy — TUNA? You never liked tuna before. As a matter of fact, I have only one can left, which I planned to use for Dad's lunch tomorrow. Well, go ahead, you can open it. I'll use what's left over for Dad."

Ahuva busied herself with the preparation of her sandwich, choosing not to explain herself for the time being. Actually, she didn't care much for tuna fish at all. But if Adina liked spaghetti and meatballs, then she would just have to start liking tuna sandwiches. After all, it wouldn't be right to ask Mom to make two different suppers every night! Wordlessly, she washed her hands for bread, and sat down at the table.

Mrs. Wein pulled up a chair next to her and sat down. "Are you sure that will fill you up?" she asked.

Ahuva nodded as she swallowed her first bite. She thought of round tasty meatballs cooked in her mother's delicious home-made spaghetti sauce, and her mouth watered.

"No salad, nothing?"

Oh, those crispy, crunchy, refreshing vegetables!

"Uh-uh. Thanks, Mom. Really, this is fine."

Suddenly, Mrs. Wein put her hand to her forehead. "Of course! Why, here I am thinking you must be starving, when I myself brought a plate of chocolate chip cookies up to your room earlier. I thought I heard you crying, so I followed you upstairs. You didn't notice me, so I just left them there."

"Thank you, Mom. I didn't eat them, though."

"Chocolate chip cookies are your favorite, aren't they?"

"Not anymore," muttered Ahuva, looking away. She was beginning to wonder if her plan was at all practical. Things were already tougher than she'd expected, and it had only been five minutes!

Mrs. Wein looked questioningly at her. "Did you and Ahuva have a fight?"

"No." It was the truth. The struggle was with herself. Adina hadn't started it.

Mrs. Wein was pensive for a while. Both of her daughters had always been encouraged to discuss their problems or worries with her. In fact, Ahuva often confided in her even more than Adina did. Today, however, her behavior had been most unusual, and she was not sharing what was on her mind.

"I'll tell you what," ventured Mrs. Wein.

"Hmmm?" Ahuva brushed a few crumbs off her hands, as she swallowed the last bite.

"There's still about a week or so left before school starts. How about a family trip to Washington, D.C.?"

"Wow!" she said without thinking. "What a neat idea! Did you ask Adina yet?"

"Ask me what? Did I hear my name?" Adina asked,

floating happily into the kitchen. She poured herself a cold drink, and joined them at the table.

"Oh, Ahuva! I'm so glad you're up. I was getting worried about you."

Ahuva shrugged. "I'm feeling better now."

"Adina," said Mrs. Wein, smiling, "you have a very considerate sister. She won't go to Washington, D.C. unless you agree to it, too."

"Wait a minute," thought Ahuva. "I hadn't meant that at all!"

"Agree? Of course I want to go to Washington, D.C. Who wouldn't?"

"Me," said Ahuva quietly.

"What?" said Adina.

"I don't want to go to Washington," Ahuva restated simply.

"I misunderstood," said Mrs. Wein quickly. "But the rest of us will be going, *Im Yirtzeh Hashem*. I'll ask Dad when he can take a few days off from work." She gazed at Ahuva quizzically. "Are you sure you don't want to come, dear?"

"Positive," said Ahuva.

"But we've always dreamed of going to Washington!" Adina said. "We've talked about and planned this trip for so long, Ahuva. I can't believe you're not coming. Please come! It won't be the same without you!"

"I've made up my mind," said Ahuva resolutely. "I'll stay with a friend for a few days."

Blinking back a tear, Adina asked, "Who? Tehillah?"

"No."

"Yocheved?"

"No."

"Who? Is it a secret?"

"Well ..." The truth was that she hadn't had much time to think about who she'd like to stay with. Everything was happening so fast!

"You'll stay with Bubby, then," said Mrs. Wein with surprising firmness.

"But —"

"She'll enjoy your company, and she's a wonderful hostess. I've got to run now. My *shiur* starts at nine o'clock. You two can play Scrabble or something until I get back." She went upstairs to get ready.

"Ahuva?" said Adina expectantly. But Ahuva said nothing.

"Come on, Ahuva. Didn't you once tell me I was your closest friend in the whole world? We've done everything together since we were babies! We've always shared our secrets and our troubles. We've always been there for one another, no matter what. All of a sudden, you don't want to have anything to do with me. At least that's what it looks like. I feel as if I'm in your way. Oh, never mind," her voice cracked as she spoke. "You're sitting there listening to me as if I'm from another planet! I hope you have fun at Bubby's 'cause I plan to have fun in Washington D.C. with Mom and Dad, even if you don't come."

With that, she got up and left the kitchen. *Even if you don't come.* The words stung. Would Adina really have fun without her? Could *she* really have fun without

Adina? What would she do all day at Bubby's house? That is, besides helping her cook and keeping her company, which she did enjoy. Gilah Abrams lives next door to Bubby, she consoled herself. Not that we've ever had much to do with each other. But at least there will be someone my age to talk to.

She *bentched* and went to the den. Restlessly, she chose a book to read, found a nice comfortable spot on the couch, and snuggled into it. No sooner had she turned to the first page than Mr. Wein walked in.

"Mom home?" he called to whoever might happen to know.

"She went to a *shiur,*" replied Ahuva, without looking up.

"Wonderful! Who's speaking?"

"Rabbi Paysach Krohn, I think. Let's see. . . Chapter One."

"Oh, he's terrific. Guess what, Ahuva? Ahuva? It's respectful to face someone who is talking to you."

Ahuva blushed. "I'm sorry, Dad."

"Forgiven. Here, take a look at these outfits I brought home for you. A business associate of mine received these free designer samples which he can't use. Isn't that *basherte?* Mom was just telling me that you girls need new outfits for *Yom Tov.*"

He lay the package on the coffee table, and opened it carefully.

"It's exquisite!" breathed Ahuva. She touched the fine delicate fabric, admiring its softly blended hues of pale lavender and peach. She and Adina both preferred light colors to match their fair appearances. She looked again. Sure enough, there were two of them, exactly alike. She couldn't refuse Adina's, but she could give up her own. After all, she'd resolved to be completely independent, hadn't she? There was no turning back now.

"I'm sure Adina will adore it," she said.

Mr. Wein looked happy. "I'm glad. The two of you will —"

"As for me, I prefer — um — darker colors," she stammered.

Recalling their conversation that afternoon, he said only, "Well then. Maybe you know someone else who could use this dress? He doesn't need the dresses back."

She thought for a brief moment, then exclaimed, "Gilah! She'll love it. I'll give it to her next time I see her."

"A *chesed* never hurt anyone," said Mr. Wein. "Oh, before these melt. . ." He took two candy bars from his pocket. "One Brunch Munch for you, and one for Adina."

Ahuva heaved a great, big sigh. Would the temptations never cease? "No, thanks. I'm on a diet," she said shakily.

"A diet? Since when?"

"Since a moment ago," she thought wryly. "Oh, today. I've got to fit into my school uniform," she said.

"Well, that's better than most people I know. They're all starting their diets *tomorrow.*" He chuckled. "It's always a day away, isn't it?" He glanced at his watch. "*Oi vey!* It's nine thirty. *Ma'ariv* is in ten minutes. Enjoy your book!" Then he left.

As if on cue, tears sprang to her eyes. Enjoy? What was there left to enjoy? She had turned down her favorite supper, her favorite candy bar, a stunning dress, and a trip of a lifetime! Worse yet, she had turned down her own dear sister. "Why am I doing this?" she pondered sadly. "I was unhappy before, but now I feel more miserable than ever!"

A tear fell onto the page of her book. She looked down. Page One, still. It seemed like the story of her life.

❦ ❦ ❦

Part Three

The walls were full of graffiti, and a long subway train clattered cacophonously overhead. Welcome to Kensington, read a weather-beaten sign at the corner.

Turning on to East Second Street, the cab driver asked, "Chere?"

Ahuva recognized the heavy Russian accent immediately. She tutored a Russian immigrant woman, so she knew a few words herself.

"*Da. Spacebo!*" (Yes. Thank you!)

The man's grin revealed several gold teeth, as he said, "*Pozholusta!* (You're welcome!) Dis your chome?'"

She fumbled in her wallet for the fare. "Home? No. *Babochka's* home."

He laughed heartily. "*Babochka* — dis is butterfly. You mean *Babushke?*"

She laughed, too. "Yes! *Babushke.*" She paid him an extra fifty cents, and stepped out of the taxi. "*Dosvedanya!*" (Goodbye!)

"Chev a goot veekend," he said. His Jewish customers were so much more courteous than some of the other passengers he met daily. He felt proud to be connected.

Ahuva's grandmother was waiting near the front gate of her pretty white house. Ahuva unlatched the gate and hugged her warmly.

"Hi, darling!" said Mrs. Silver. "Oh, it's so good to see you, sweetheart! You know, you look so much like your mother did when she was your age. It's amazing, the similarity. Well, come on in. I've even got lunch prepared for us. I tried to remember all your favorite foods. . ." Her voice trailed off as she went ahead of Ahuva into the house. Ahuva followed, slowly. How excited everyone had been this morning as Dad packed up the car for the trip to Washington, D.C. She tried to block the scene from her mind.

Bubby's house was perfectly kept, warm, and oh, so inviting!

"Come, honey, let's put your things down in the green room." Her eyes twinkled. "Remember the green room?"

"I sure do!" said Ahuva, trying to sound cheerful. It would be the first time she wasn't sharing the green room with Adina. It would be the first time she wouldn't be staying up half the night, poring over old family albums with Adina.

"Ahuva? Is everything all right?"

"Sure!"

"You've been staring at the beds as if you were afraid I'd put a frog in one of them," Bubby said, with her kind, gentle laugh.

"Oh, but I like frogs!" she joked good-naturedly. "I know, I'm tired, Bubby. I stayed up late last night packing. So I'm a little out of it."

"That's okay, darling. Why don't you leave your duffel bag here, and join me for lunch?"

"I'd love to," said Ahuva, as they entered the dining room. The table was set for two, on a dazzlingly white tablecloth, with Bubby's finest china and silverware.

"Wow!" exclaimed Ahuva. "You must be expecting some important company. Aren't these your *Shabbos* dishes?"

Bubby's soft, brown eyes shone as she replied, "Oh, I am. Or rather, I was. My important company has just arrived!"

Ahuva looked towards the front door. "Where? Oh, you mean *me?* Wow!" She shook her head in disbelief. "I can't believe it, Bubby. You've never used your *Shabbos* dishes on Thursdays, even for the family!"

"Well," explained Bubby, "when *all* of you come from Toronto, I use plastic dishes and cutlery. All those dishes would be too much for me to wash. But it's just you and I, so why not?"

"Oh, Bubby, you are the best!" declared Ahuva earnestly.

"Aren't all Bubbies? Come, let's wash before everything gets cold."

A few minutes later, they sat down to eat. Ahuva found herself surrounded by all kinds of sumptuous delicacies which Bubby had cooked for the occasion.

"When did you do all this?" she asked incredulously.

Bubby put her finger to her lips. "Don't talk when you eat, honey," she said, with a mischievous smile. "Just relax and enjoy."

Dessert was chocolate mousse with whipped cream and fresh strawberries served on the side, a childhood favorite of the twins.

"I don't deserve all this, Bubby," said Ahuva, licking the last bit of mousse from her spoon.

"Oh, don't be silly, dear. Of course you do!"

"I've been awful to everyone lately. I feel crummy about myself, I really do!"

Bubby placed both hands on either side of her head, covering her ears. "It hurts my ears to hear you say that, darling. Such a beautiful, kind-hearted, talented girl as you should never feel that way. Has someone — "

"No, it's me, only me. And I don't know *what* to do anymore." She stopped suddenly, swallowing the last syllable of the word.

"Go on," said Bubby patiently. "We've got all the time in the world."

"It's just that — oh, great. I'm going to start crying now, just like a baby. I wish these stupid tears wouldn't — "

"Relax, honey. I love you and care about you. Let the tears come, Ahuva. I promise that I won't think one bit less of you."

"What ridiculous timing," thought Ahuva, struggling with the tears that threatened to spill over any minute. She tried with all her might to hold them back. She felt so foolish and ashamed! "I'm sorry to spoil this special meal," she said in a choked voice.

"You haven't spoiled anything, honey. The meal is over. Tell me what's bothering you, Ahuva. Maybe I can help."

The lump in her throat was getting bigger, and she no longer trusted her voice. Would Bubby understand? Would she think Ahuva was being childish and silly?

"I won't judge you," said Bubby calmly, as if reading her mind.

Just then, the doorbell rang.

"I'll get it," said Bubby. "It might be Gilah. Shall I tell her to come back later?"

"No, I'll be okay," said Ahuva. She wanted to get her mind off of all this anyway.

"Are you sure, sweetheart?"

Ahuva nodded, and Bubby went to open the front door.

"Is Ahuva here yet?" asked a deep, hoarse voice. "It is definitely Gilah," thought Ahuva. She got up and walked over to her.

"Howdy, Twin," Gilah said, smiling self-consciously.

"Hi, Gilah. Come on in," said Ahuva. Why was it such an effort to sound happy? "I'll just *bentch* and — oh, I brought you a present from Toronto! Mind waiting?"

"No. Is it okay if I sit on the couch here, Mrs. Silver?"

"Of course. Make yourself at home."

Ahuva tried hard to concentrate on *birchas hamazon*. She knew that Gilah was watching her and felt slightly uncomfortable.

Gilah was tall and thin, lanky almost. Her dark brown hair was long and dull looking. Her face was red, and beads of perspiration framed her forehead and mouth. Ahuva felt sorry for her, for she knew that Gilah was shy and had very few friends, if any.

"I'll clear the table, don't you worry," said Bubby, putting down her own *bentcher*. "Gilah can keep you company in the green room, as you unpack." She turned to Gilah. "Are all teenagers alike? Going away for a weekend, and bringing enough clothes to last a month?"

"I wouldn't know," said Gilah, looking away as she spoke. "I only *have* a few outfits, so I don't do that."

"Oh," said Bubby quietly. "Well, it makes doing laundry a lot easier, doesn't it?"

"Not really, Mrs. Silver. My mother takes all our clothing to the laundromat. We can't afford a washing machine or dryer."

Poor Bubby! Ahuva cleared her throat, loudly. "Come, Gilah. I'd better unpack before everything gets wrinkled."

Mrs. Silver watched as Gilah followed Ahuva down the hallway towards the green room, head bent and shoulders slouched. She seemed to be dragging one foot in front of the other, as if walking took an effort she could hardly expend. "Tall girls must mind their posture," she thought, but held her tongue.

Gilah sat down on one of the beds, biting her nails as Ahuva unzipped her duffel bag.

"Well, what dooo you know?" said Ahuva dramatically, holding up the lavender and peach dress for Gilah to see. "All the way from Toronto, Canada! Going once, going twice — gone! To the lady in the brown skirt —"

"It's not brown. It's beige," corrected Gilah. "It drives me crazy when people call it brown."

"I stand corrected," continued Ahuva. She knew better than to argue with Gilah. "The lady in the beige skirt and mustard T-shirt is the winner!"

"Mustard?"

"Yeah, it's a shade of yellow."

"My shirt is yellow, thank you. I hate mustard."

"Anyway, here's the dress, Gilah. Isn't it just gorgeous?"

"You mean it's for me? Wowee. I thought you were joking."

"No, it's for you. Don't you love it?"

"Seriously? You bought this for me? No way!"

Ahuva put the dress down, and placed both hands squarely on her hips. "Now, why would I lie to you, Gilah? Come on, try it on. I bet you'll look great in it."

"That's impossible," said Gilah. "You and your sister are so pretty, and I'm sure you're really popular over there in Toronto. I, on the other hand. . ."

Ahuva sat down on the bed opposite Gilah. "You look nice," she said pleasantly. She felt as if she were walking on a tightrope; one wrong step and she'd fall into the abyss below.

"Nice?!"

One wrong word. She waited for the torrent of words that was sure to follow.

"You call this nice? I've got oily hair, plain grey eyes, and the worst case of acne in history. I'm usually pale, and my mother says that all my clothes are "blah." I'll look like a joke in that dress. It's — it's *too* nice for me. Why don't *you* keep it, anyway?''

''Next time I'll bring you stationery,'' said Ahuva, half-seriously. She tried to change the topic, and asked, ''How's your family?''

''Oh, don't ask,'' answered Gilah, biting her nails again. ''It's been one thing after another. First, my father lost his job, and now my mother's flat on her back, in bed. My brothers tease me all the time. The only good that has happened to us since I last saw you is that my aunt and uncle moved back from Israel. But they don't give two hoots about me, anyway. Our friendship is a one-way street. I admire them, but that's where it ends.''

''What do you mean?''

''Well, I'm always begging them to let me babysit for their baby, but they always have excuses why I shouldn't. I know it's 'cause they don't like me, but I never tell them that I know.''

Ahuva shook her head. Her heart went out to Gilah, and she tried to be understanding.

''I'm sorry to hear that. Well, anything exciting going on in school? I mean, school is over — but, camp?''

''You *know* I never go to camp in the summer. We barely have enough money for tuition during the year. Forget about camp!''

''Adina and I didn't go to camp this summer either, so don't feel bad. Actually, we both took jobs as counselors in the day camp for six weeks. Yesterday was our last day.''

''Yeah, I'm a counselor, too,'' said Gilah, playing with a

long strand of hair. "I hate every minute of it, though. The kids are so bratty, you wouldn't believe it. All day, they pester me. 'Can I play with your hair? Why do you have dots all over your face?' I can't wait until camp is over. It's not even worth the money."

Ahuva was getting a headache. Something was very wrong here, but she couldn't place her finger on it. After all, they were just having a friendly chat, weren't they? She decided to change the subject.

"You know, you've been such good company, Gilah. I've unpacked my whole duffel bag, without even realizing the time going by! Really, it was so thoughtful of you to stop in."

Gilah looked down at her toes. It was obvious that she was unused to any kind of praise, and didn't know how to react.

Just then, on an impulse, Ahuva said, "How would you like to have a sleep-over party tonight? If my grand-mother doesn't mind, of course."

Gilah's whole face lit up. "Boy, I wish you lived here, Ahuva. This is the first invitation I've ever gotten to a slumber party in my life! Nobody ever invites me to anything, and my only friend isn't allowed to have sleep-over parties at her house."

"Is that a yes?" asked Ahuva. She tried to sound enthusiastic.

"I'll ask my parents. I'm sure they'll let, though. Anything to get me out of their hair."

"Great! I'll ask my grandmother, and I'll phone you later, okay?"

For the second time since the beginning of her visit, Gilah smiled. "Thanks! Thanks for coming to New York!"

Ahuva smiled back. "I'll call," she said, as Gilah stood up to leave. She accompanied her to the front door, where Bubby was watering some plants.

"Regards to your mother, Gilah," said Bubby politely.

"Okay," said Gilah, leaving. "Bye."

"Bubby?" said Ahuva, as the door closed behind her guest.

"Yes, honey?"

"Can we still talk?"

"Of course we can, Ahuva. I'm nearly finished. There, that's the last plant." She looked around, surveying her living room with pride. "So, how do you like my indoor garden?"

"It's really nice," replied Ahuva, not without admiration. "Every time I buy a plant, it withers. If Adina doesn't water it, it doesn't get watered. I never remember to water it. Do you think that might have something to do with its dying?" she asked, giggling.

"Of course," said Bubby. "I take very good care of my plants. They need sunshine, water and vitamins to grow properly, and I don't neglect any of them."

"They look very well groomed," said Ahuva, fingering the velvety texture of a deep green leaf.

"Even natural beauty needs care," said Bubby.

Ahuva was quiet for a moment. "Thanks, Bubby. That's exactly what I'll say."

"To whom?"

"To Gilah. Those words are beautiful." She paused. "Can Gilah sleep over tonight, Bubby?"

"Certainly. The green room can be very lonely with one empty bed." She went to empty the watering can in the sink. "Care for a drink?" she called, opening the refrigerator.

"Sure. Thanks," Ahuva answered, dropping tiredly on the couch.

Bubby reappeared with two tall glasses of orange juice, crackling with ice. She placed one glass gently on the lamp table, and sat down with the other drink in her hand.

"So, what made you decide to give up Washington, D.C.?" she asked, sipping slowly.

"I thought it was the only way," began Ahuva. "At first, that is. I've been trying to pretend that Adina and I are no longer twins, and that we don't like the same things."

"Really?"

"Yeah. It's involved some difficult decisions, but I've stayed strong."

"It's an interesting idea," said Bubby thoughtfully. "What made you think of it?"

"Well, I've been feeling that people don't realize that Adina and I are two separate people, with separate feelings and personalities."

"Of course! Even though you have quite a bit in common, you've got many of your own individual qualities, too. I think anyone who knows you well knows that."

"But it's the people who know us best who always seem to be lumping us together as if we were one person."

"How is that?"

"In school, the girls say, 'Oh, let's ask the Wein twins,' or 'Let's invite Adina and Ahuva to study with us.' We get identical gifts for our birthdays. Things like that."

"What else?"

"We share everything at home. Our room, our clothes. We do homework together, and visit people together."

"Do you enjoy each other's company?"

"I guess we do. We understand each other very well. We're always on the same side, whatever happens."

"Loyalty," said Bubby. "Your mother and Aunt Sheila were like that, too. They couldn't bear to be apart from one another!"

"Well, I guess that's why Mom doesn't really understand me." She sighed sadly.

"See that picture hanging above the fireplace?" asked Bubby, pointing to an old framed photograph on the ledge. "That's your great-grandmother, my mother. Her name was Ahuva. I was thrilled when you were named after her." She gazed lovingly at the picture. "She was a very wise woman, my mother. Do you know what she often told me when I complained? She'd say, 'Mame'le, when nobody understands you — neither your parents nor your friends — see if you understand yourself. Sometimes, there's a reason why *nobody* understands.'" She paused, letting Ahuva digest the full meaning of what she had just told her.

Ahuva thought hard. "Understand myself? Of course I understand myself. I want to be my own individual self, that's all. I want to have my own favorite foods, my own taste in clothing, my own friends, and do my own things. That's why I've been eating sandwiches for supper, and wearing plain navy and maroon all the time.

When Nobody Understands / 119

That's why I didn't go to Washington, D.C., and that's why I haven't visited Tehillah and Yocheved, or even phoned. That's why I'm here at Bubby's, and that's why I've had to listen to Gilah's depressing stories all afternoon.

"That's why I feel miserable!" she concluded aloud.

Bubby sat up straight, startled. "Go ahead," she said gently, settling back into the sofa.

"Of course, Bubby, Mom and Dad *do* know me best. So do Tehillah and Yocheved, and all of our friends. Adina can read me like a book. What's wrong with eating the same suppers and wearing the same styles? Or liking the same people? We have fun together with our friends, and they know we're close, so they invite us to places together!"

Bubby tried to clarify Ahuva's jumbled feelings. "Even though you're twins, you do have a right to express your differences. If you *prefer* something different, say so. Nicely, of course. You don't *have* to like all the same things. But since you happen to do so most of the time anyway, say *Baruch Hashem!* How convenient! Imagine if you *were* total opposites. You'd probably be arguing constantly. The way it is, you hardly have any reason to disagree with each other, see?"

"It's funny," said Ahuva, feeling as though a stone had been lifted off her chest, "I thought nobody understood me. Actually, everybody understood *but* me!"

Bubby smiled, "Nevertheless, I'm glad you didn't go to Washington. Otherwise, we wouldn't have had this wonderful chance to talk!"

The phone rang. Ahuva jumped up. "I'll get it." She spoke into the phone briefly, and hung up. "Bubby?"

"Let me guess. It's Gilah, and she's coming over after supper. Am I right?"

"You always are, Bubby." She meant it. "I just hope I can help Gilah the way you've helped me."

"You'll think of something. I have faith in you, Ahuva."

❦ ❦ ❦

Part Four

"It's a good thing your grandmother sleeps upstairs," said Gilah, as they sat cross-legged on the pale green carpet of their room.

"I hope she didn't hear us scream when the top of the popcorn popper flew off!" giggled Ahuva. She felt light-headed and happy now that her problem had been solved. She and Gilah had looked at pictures, made popcorn, enjoyed a tiring pillow-fight, and were now relaxing on the floor of the green room.

"What time is it?" asked Gilah.

"Oh, much too early to go to sleep," said Ahuva, glancing lazily at her watch. "It's only — wow! It's two A.M. Can you believe it?"

"We've talked for hours!" said Gilah. "You know, I'm glad you came to your grandmother alone this time. I've never opened up to anyone before. When you're here with your sister, I feel so — I don't know, intimidated by both of you."

"Do I look scaaary?" growled Ahuva, spreading her fingers, as if to pounce on Gilah.

Gilah laughed. "I almost wished you did, sometimes," she said, "so I wouldn't be the only one."

"You don't look scary," said Ahuva. "Wait!" She jumped up. "I have a great idea. I'm going to make you look like a queen."

"Hah," said Gilah, standing up, "Queen of the Monsters, you mean."

"Oh, please," said Ahuva impatiently. "Come. We're going to wet your hair in the sink." She practically dragged Gilah into the kitchen and had her head face-up in the sink, before she could protest. Humming crazily, she lathered a handful of shampoo, then conditioner, into Gilah's long, unwashed hair.

"Okay, out of the water!" she called, in a stage whisper, so as not to wake Bubby up. They tiptoed back into the green room.

"Just you wait and see," said Ahuva excitedly, blowing Gilah's hair this way and that.

"Ouch! You're pulling my hair out!" cried Gilah, as Ahuva styled, yanking at knots without mercy.

She stepped back to take a look. "Perfect! Now, wipe your face with these cotton balls dipped in alcohol."

"My face is so embarrassingly ugly," muttered Gilah, but she complied with surprising obedience. Ahuva bounded over to one of the drawers.

"In five minutes, I'll have this makeup on you," she said, not waiting for permission. "Oh, you look so pretty!" she exclaimed delightedly.

Gilah's clear grey eyes shone with joy. "Me, pretty? Could it be? Nah," she thought. "Ahuva's just having fun. I'll go along with it. Why not?"

"That bathrobe just won't do," said Ahuva decisively.

"Here. Put this dress on. It's yours, remember?" She handed her the lavender and peach dress she had brought from Toronto, and turned around. "Oh, what size shoe are you? Six or seven?"

"One minute, please!" begged Gilah, as she pulled the dress on over her robe. "Um. . .size seven."

"Okay, wear my *Shabbos* shoes. They're a size six, but they need stretching. Go ahead, try them on. You can't wear a dress like that with those fuzzy-wuzzy slippers!"

"This is nuts!" said Gilah. "It's almost three in the morning. I can't believe I'm letting you do this to me!" But her face was radiantly rosy, and she was enjoying every minute of the special attention Ahuva was showering on her.

"Are you ready?" asked Ahuva.

Ahuva opened the closet, and led her to the full-length mirror nailed inside the door. "There! Take a look!"

Gilah gasped. She could barely speak. "I hardly recognize myself," she whispered.

"You look absolutely smashing!" declared Ahuva, joining her. She put an arm around Gilah, and said, "Gorgeous Gilah. You see? Anything is possible."

"I — I never thought I could look good," said Gilah, not taking her eyes off the mirror. "I wish I could do it again for my parents."

"You can," said Ahuva seriously. "Just wash your face every day, keep your hair clean — you know. As my grandmother says, 'Even natural beauty needs care.' "

"I bet I'd have a lot more friends if I took better care of myself," said Gilah.

"There's a lot more to friendship than just looks,'" said Ahuva, pulling her gently away from the mirror. "People like to be around happy people. Smile a lot. Say yes a lot. Don't tell everyone everything every time. See that sign on the wall? I made it in school when I was nine years old. My grandmother hangs up everything we send her."

"Which one? That small poster in the corner?"

"Uh huh. It says: עִבְדוּ אֶת ה׳ בְּשִׂמְחָה. It's a *mitzvah* to be happy. If a person complains all the time, people don't enjoy his company. Oh, listen to me. Going on and on like this. It's just that I'm sure you have it in you, Gilah."

Gilah raised her hand, as if in class. "Can I say something?"

"Of course! I've been talking for hours, haven't I?"

"No. I mean, maybe you have, but I don't mind." There was a flicker of confidence in her clear grey eyes as she spoke. "You know what your grandmother once told me?"

"*My* grandmother?"

"Yes, I talk to her sometimes. She said, 'Whenever nobody understands you — neither your parents nor your friends — see if you understand yourself. Sometimes, there's a reason why *nobody* understands.' "

Ahuva's eyes opened wide.

"It sounded right when she said it," Gilah went on. "But I never really understood what she meant.

Until tonight. I'll never forget what you've done for me, Ahuva. I finally understand, and it's thanks to you.''

Ahuva smiled, and leaned over to squeeze Gilah's hand, her heart surging with pure joy. Washington, D.C. couldn't come close to this. She was certain of that.

❀ ❀ ❀

Tamar Books publishes
novels and young people's
literature on Judaic themes.
The Tamar imprint is
your assurance of reading pleasure,
good taste and literary quality.

For current publications
visit your local Hebrew bookseller
or contact the publisher:

Tamar
Books
4401 Second Ave.
Brooklyn, N.Y. 11232
(718) 921-9000